book *of* faith
Lenten Journey

book *of* faith
Lenten Journey
Seven Wonders of the Word

Kathryn A. Kleinhans

BOOK OF FAITH LENTEN JOURNEY
Seven Wonders of the Word

Text on pages 7–19 adapted from David L. Miller, *Book of Faith Lenten Journey: Marks of the Christian* (Augsburg Fortress, 2009); Henry F. French, *Book of Faith Lenten Journey: 40 Days with the Lord's Prayer* (Augsburg Fortress, 2009); and Ron Klug, *How to Keep a Spiritual Journal* (Augsburg Books, 1993).

For information on the Book of Faith initiative and Book of Faith resources, go to www.bookoffaith.org.

Book of Faith is an initiative of the

 Evangelical Lutheran Church in America
God's work. Our hands.

Cover design: Joe Vaughan
Interior design: Ivy Palmer Skrade, Joe Vaughan
Typesetting: PerfecType, Nashville, TN

ISBN 978-1-4514-0096-0

Manufactured in the U.S.A.

14   13   12   3   4   5   6   7   8   9   10

Contents

Our Writer

Kathryn A. Kleinhans serves as Professor of Religion at Wartburg College, Waverly, Iowa. Her scholarly expertise is the theology of Martin Luther and the Lutheran Confessions. Whether in scholarly publications, popular articles, or devotional writings, she is passionate about making Lutheran theological insights relevant for Christians today.

Preface

Book of Faith, an initiative of the Evangelical Lutheran Church in America (ELCA), affirms the centrality of the Bible to Christian life and faith, while recognizing the lack of biblical literacy in the church. The initial Book of Faith Web site addressed this issue of biblical literacy as one of biblical fluency:

> The Book of Faith initiative invites the whole church to become more fluent in the first language of faith, the language of Scripture, in order that we might live into our calling as a people renewed, enlivened, empowered and sent by the Word.
>
> The Bible is the written Word of God that creates and nurtures faith through the work of the Holy Spirit and points us to Christ, the incarnate Word and center of our faith. The Bible invites us into a relationship with God, making demands on our lives and promising us life in Christ. The Bible tells the stories of people living their faith over the centuries and, through its demands and promises, forms us as a people of faith.
>
> The language of the Bible becomes our language. It shapes how we think and speak about God, about the world, and about ourselves. We become renewed, enlivened, and empowered as the language of Scripture forms our hearts, our minds, our community conversation, and our commitments.

The goal of the Book of Faith initiative is to increase our engagement, individually and collectively, with the Bible and its teachings, resulting in increased biblical fluency and appreciation of Lutheran principles and approaches for reading and understanding Scripture. *Book of Faith Lenten Journey: Seven Wonders of the Word* is one of many resources prepared to accomplish this goal.

This book will engage you in an encounter with the active power of the Word of God. Each week the journey uses scriptural passages to explore one of the many ways God's Word is at work in the world and in our lives.

You can use *Book of Faith Lenten Journey: Seven Wonders of the Word* on your own, together with a spiritual friend or small group, or with your entire congregation. Related worship helps and sermon starters for Sundays and Wednesday evenings in Lent are available online at www.bookoffaith.org. Be sure to visit the Book of Faith Web site regularly for more resources designed to bring the book of faith and the community of faith closer together.

Introduction

The theme "Seven Wonders of the Word" is, in part, a play on the Seven Wonders of the World, attractions of great beauty and also of great skill and design. Travelers in the ancient world were awestruck at the sight of them. Few were able to visit all seven in their lifetimes. Focusing on the Seven Wonders of the Word, rather than the world, gives us the opportunity to see and experience the Scriptures from a new perspective and, we hope, to be deeply moved by them as we encounter their great beauty and their great power.

Often when we read and reflect on the Scriptures, we think of ourselves as the subjects and the Scriptures as the object of our study and devotion. *Seven Wonders of the Word* reverses that familiar pattern, making the Word itself the active subject of our Lenten journey. Each week has a theme, and all seven themes are phrased as verbs. The Word creates, calls, commands, saves, sustains, shapes, and sends. Note that it is the Word that does the work. We, the readers, are the ones being acted upon: created, called, commanded, saved, sustained, shaped, and sent.

This focus on the activity of God's Word is not new for Lutherans. The Augsburg Confession, a document written during the Reformation to present the beliefs of Martin Luther and his followers, identifies the Word and the sacraments as "means of grace." Think of similar phrases we use, such as "means of communication" or "means of transportation." These phrases reflect the assumption that things need to happen and that there are multiple ways in which those things can happen. Telephone, e-mail, a loving look—these are all means or ways by which communication takes place. Bicycle, airplane, automobile, walking—these are all means or methods of moving from one location to another. By calling Word and sacrament "means of grace," Lutheran Christians express the conviction that these are two ways through which God really and prayer. You may want to keep a hymnal with your copy of this book so that you can easily read or sing the rest of these hymns, if you wish.

Begin your journey with this blessing: "Let the word of Christ dwell in you richly; teach and admonish one another in all wisdom; and with gratitude in your hearts sing psalms, hymns, and spiritual songs to God" (Colossians 3:16).

How to Use This Book

Your forty-day Lenten journey into *Seven Wonders of the Word* will challenge you to experience the power of God's Word in your life and in our world. It will expand your awareness of what God is saying and doing. It will also encourage you to deepen your prayer life as you relate the power of God's Word to your personal experience.

You will benefit most by finding a regular time during the day to work through this book. It is easier to maintain a spiritual practice if you do it at the same time each day. Mornings are best for many people. The home and heart are still quiet and the busyness of the day has not yet distracted the mind. Others find that the noon hour or before bedtime are better for them. Do whatever works for you to maintain a regular, daily encounter with God and God's Word.

You will note that there are no readings for Sunday. The forty days of Lent traditionally exclude Sundays, the day we celebrate the resurrection of Christ.

Although this book is designed to be used during the forty days of Lent, it can be used at any time of the year. If you pick a time other than Lent for your journey, it would still be best to walk day-by-day through the book. Each day's devotion offers plenty of rich resources for you to ponder. There is no need to rush. For this reason, if you are not able to read through *Seven Wonders of the Word* in forty days, feel free to slow down and take a longer period of time. It is better to complete the journey at your own pace than to give it up partway through. Set a schedule that works for you and be as consistent as you can.

Each day's journey contains several elements, including great riches of faith, experience, and the witness of faithful Christians who have gone before us. Sometimes you may find it fruitful to spend more than one day with a particular reflection, question, or quotation that stirs you. If one element speaks more deeply to you than others—blessing, challenging, or troubling you—spend time with it. Always go where there is fruit. Don't worry that the other elements don't touch your mind and heart that day. Go where Christ is pleased to speak and give himself to you. Luther wrote, "If you pause here and let him do you good, that is if you believe that he benefits and helps you, then you really have it. The Christ is yours, presented to you as a gift."[2]

Consider bringing a notebook or journal with you on this journey. Jot down questions and insights, graces and blessings, challenges and changes in your life as they bubble up in you.

Each week the journey spotlights a different verb to guide our exploration of the wonders of the Word. In some weeks the focus is addressed by digging deeply into a single Scriptural passage for the entire week, examining a verse or two each day. For these weeks, I encourage you to reread the entire passage, provided on the introductory page for that week, before reading the daily devotion. This will set the day's verse in context and prompt you to make connections throughout the week. In other weeks, several different passages are used to explore the theme.

Each day of the journey begins with a biblical verse, followed by a brief reflection on that verse. These daily reflections are intended to stir your own thinking and meditation, so read slowly. You may want to read through each reflection more than once, perhaps even reading it aloud so that it can speak to your ears as well as your eyes. Let the words sink into your consciousness. Take time to consider and benefit from what God is saying to you and in you.

Following the daily reflection, you will find the heading *Biblical Wisdom* and a brief passage from another place in the Scriptures that relates to the meditation. It may be obvious to you how this second passage relates to the day's theme, or you may need to think about it for a while before you make a connection. Either way, read the biblical text slowly. Let it speak to you.

After the second scriptural passage, you will find *Theological Thoughts*. These brief quotations from other Christians—saints and mystics, scholars and theologians from throughout Christian history—expand upon thoughts and experiences in the reflections.

Next comes the heading *Silence for Meditation*. Here you might spend anywhere from five to twenty minutes meditating on the readings. Begin by getting centered. Sit with your back straight, eyes closed, hands folded in your lap, and breathe slowly and deeply. Remember that breath is a gift from God, the gift of life. Do nothing but observe your breath for two or three minutes. Focus your awareness on the end of your nose or your hands in your lap. Feel the breath (life) enter . . . and leave . . . through your nostrils. Each breath draws in God's gracious decision that you "may have life, and have it abundantly" (John 10:10).

Once you feel yourself settling down, open your eyes and slowly look over the daily meditation, the scriptural passages, and the theological thought again. Note the words, thoughts, images, and feelings that draw you. Explore meanings and implications for your life. Jot down any insights that occur to you. Do the readings raise questions for you? Write them down. Do the readings suggest some action or response? Write it down.

Stay with the meditation time as long as it feels useful. When your mind is ready to move on, close your eyes, observe your breath for a minute, and thank God for the gift of life and the gift of God's Word.

Then move on to the *Psalm Fragment*. The Psalms have been a mainstay of prayer for Jewish and Christian believers, speaking the deepest hope, joy, and pain of our lives.

Pray the *Psalm Fragment*, silently or aloud, and reflect for a moment before continuing to *Questions to Ponder*. Here you will find several questions related to the day's readings. The questions use the insights of the readings to draw you into your own experience, so you may see where and how God is working in your life and in our world. These questions may be used for personal reflection, as a basis for conversation with others, and as prompts to respond to in your journal. It is helpful to jot down a few quick notes as your first response to the questions before sharing your thoughts with others in conversation or developing them at more length in your journal. You need not answer every question. Choose those that draw you or evoke thought, memory, or emotion. The questions provided in this book may also lead you to ask new questions. Again, go where there is fruit.

Journaling as a spiritual practice can be profoundly transforming. It can keep us more closely in touch with ourselves and our response to God over time. Sometimes we don't really know or understand our thoughts and feelings until we write them down and look at what flows from the pen or through our fingers on the keyboard. We may be surprised to see what is actually moving and happening in us. Then we can draw insight and consolation from what God is saying and doing. In the next section, you will find some suggestions for how to keep a journal.

On the last day of each week, you will see an additional section called *More Questions to Ponder*. These questions are the same every week. Based on a spiritual practice developed by Ignatius of Loyola, called the "examination of conscience" or the "examination of consciousness," they are intended to help you identify patterns that develop in your faith life over the course of this seven-week journey with the Word.

The final heading is *Prayer for Today*, a one- or two-line prayer to end your session. You might choose to repeat this prayer from time to time throughout the day.

Hints on Keeping a Journal

A journal is a helpful tool for many people. Keeping a journal can also be a form of prayer, a powerful way of getting to know yourself—and God—more deeply. Journaling helps you focus and clarify your thoughts, while keeping a record of your insights, questions, and prayers. It may lead you to thoughts and awareness that will surprise you. As you write, you can respond to God with your thanks and pleas, your joys and sorrows, offering them all to God. Although you could read *Seven Wonders of the Word* and simply reflect on it in your head, consider journaling through this Lenten journey.

1. Write freely. Ignore your inner critic. Don't worry about grammar, literary style, whether you are writing in complete sentences, or what it sounds like. Just write! Simply get in touch with an idea, emotion, image, or memory and begin writing. Describe what you notice, how you feel, and how something is affecting you. From time to time, read back over your words to notice what is happening more clearly.

2. Be honest with God. Do not censor yourself! Don't write what you think you're supposed to believe or feel or think. Don't write what you think is acceptable to your spouse or friends, your pastor, or your fourth-grade teacher. Write your real thoughts, feelings, beliefs, and experiences as far as you can identify them. When you are uncertain, write your confusion and questions. Your relationship with God will be as real and honest as you are.

3. Begin and end your journaling with prayer. Ask for insight to see God's work more clearly, to notice what is really going on beneath the surface of your days and thoughts. At the end, thank God for the guidance, wisdom, or consolation that has come through your writing.

4. Feel free to address God directly in your writing. You may choose to write your entire journal entry as a prayer. Share what is happening to you and in you, what you are noticing in your journey with this book. Like the psalmists and Job, hold nothing back. You will be surprised by what bubbles out of you.

5. Don't worry or stop if your journaling takes you in directions beyond the suggestions in this book. Go where you are led. Notice what you notice. The Holy Spirit will lead you to places where you may drink from the living waters Christ Jesus offers. This book's journaling ideas and *Questions to Ponder* are suggestions for your writing. Don't hesitate to move in other directions when promising avenues appear.

6. You may wish to carry this book and your notebook or journal with you every day during your journey (only keep them safe from prying eyes). Your Lenten journey is an intense experience that doesn't stop when you close the book. When your mind and heart are stirred during the day, it is helpful to be able to write notes or new journal entries as thoughts or feelings occur to you.

Journeying with Others

You can use this book (and I hope you do) with another person or with a small group. It is best for each person first to do his or her own reading, reflection, and writing in solitude. When you come together, share the insights you have gained from your time alone. Your discussion can focus on any of the elements of each day's journey.

Questions to Ponder is a natural place to start discussions with a group or spiritual friend. However, you might find that a section from a daily reflection, *Biblical Wisdom*, or *Theological Thoughts* has stirred you or members of your group. If so, start there, and let the discussion flow in the directions that are most fruitful for the needs and questions of the group. Trust that God's Word will bear good fruit in your conversation.

If you are working through the book with people you trust, you may feel comfortable sharing some of what you have written in your journal. But no one should ever be pressured to do this. It should also be a ground rule that whatever is said in a small group stays in the group.

Always remember that your goal is to grow in relation with Christ and his church and in your understanding of God's Word. You gather to learn from one another, not to argue or to prove that you are right and the other is wrong. Practice listening and trying to understand why your discussion partner or small-group members think as they do.

Sharing your experiences is a way of encouraging and guiding one another. It provides the opportunity to offer feedback gently and to help one another translate insight into action.

By all means, pray together. This strengthens the spiritual bonds among those who take the journey together. Spend a few moments sharing prayer requests around the theme of the day. Then pray for one another and your faith community as you bring your time together to a close.

Journey Week One: The Word Creates

Day 1 and Days 4–6

In the beginning when God created the heavens and the earth, the earth was a formless void and darkness covered the face of the deep, while a wind from God swept over the face of the waters. Then God said, "Let there be light"; and there was light. And God saw that the light was good; and God separated the light from the darkness. God called the light Day, and the darkness he called Night. And there was evening and there was morning, the first day.

. . . Then God said, "Let us make humankind in our image, according to our likeness; and let them have dominion over the fish of the sea, and over the birds of the air, and over the cattle, and over all the wild animals of the earth, and over every creeping thing that creeps upon the earth."

So God created humankind in his image, in the image of God he created them; male and female he created them.

God blessed them, and God said to them, "Be fruitful and multiply, and fill the earth and subdue it; and have dominion over the fish of the sea and over the birds of the air and over every living thing that moves upon the earth."

. . . God saw everything that he had made, and indeed, it was very good.
And there was evening and there was morning, the sixth day.
    Genesis 1:1-5, 26-28, 31

Days 2–3

In the beginning was the Word, and the Word was with God, and the
Word was God. He was in the beginning with God. All things came into
being through him, and without him not one thing came into being. What
has come into being in him was life, and the life was the light of all people.
    John 1:1-4

Day 1—Ash Wednesday

> *In the beginning when God created the heavens and the earth, the earth*
> *was a formless void and darkness covered the face of the deep, while*
> *a wind from God swept over the face of the waters. Then God said, "Let*
> *there be light"; and there was light.*
>   Genesis 1:1-3

Every journey has a beginning. Our Lenten journey takes us back to the very beginning, the creation story. The Scriptures themselves are the story of people on a journey: a journey with God, a journey from a garden paradise to a heavenly city, the New Jerusalem.

Some stories begin with the storyteller's familiar phrase "Once upon a time." Our story begins with God's creative command "Let there be." God speaks, and the story begins. God speaks, and day by day, bit by bit, the entire universe comes into existence. God speaks, and God's Word creates what it names.

We underestimate God if we think the creation story only lasts for a week. Ours is no absentee god who creates the world and then leaves it to fend for itself. In the Apostles' Creed, when we confess our faith in God as the "creator of heaven and earth," we are not talking only about what God did "in the beginning." We are also describing the present relationship between God and God's created world. We never say, "God was the Creator," but always, "God is the Creator." God continues to speak to the creation, and through the Word, God continues to give life to the creation, today and every day.

In the Ash Wednesday liturgy, we hear the words "Remember that you are dust, and to dust you shall return." That's an organic description of creaturely death and decay, but it is not the final word. God's Word created us from the dust of the earth, and it is God's Word that will raise us up from the dust of the grave. Between the dawn of creation and the final day, God continues to be with us on this earthly journey. Thanks be to God!

Biblical Wisdom
"And remember, I am with you always, to the end of the age."
  Matthew 28:20b

Theological Thoughts
"Since the divine life is essentially creative, all three modes of time must be used in symbolizing it. God *has* created the world, he *is* creative in the present moment, and he *will* creatively fulfill his *telos* [goal or purpose]."[3]
  Paul Tillich

Silence for Meditation

Psalm Fragment
*By the word of the L*ord *the heavens were made,*
 and all their host by the breath of his mouth.
  Psalm 33:6

Questions to Ponder
- If you think about creation as something that is still happening today, what do you notice about the world around you? Where do you discern God's presence?
- What message does the world need to hear from its Creator today? Finish the sentence: "Let there be _____."

Prayer for Today
I thank you, God, for if you can create the entire world out of nothing, you can surely make something out of me. Amen.

Day 2—Thursday

In the beginning was the Word, and the Word was with God, and the Word was God.
  John 1:1

The opening sentence of John's Gospel is both familiar and poetic. It is also very different from the beginning of the other three Gospels. Matthew reports the genealogy of Jesus. Luke tells the stories of the unexpected pregnancies of Elizabeth and Mary. Mark fast-forwards to Jesus' adulthood and describes the beginning of Jesus' ministry. But John gives us poetry—poetry that takes us all the way back to the creation. John, like the author of Genesis, begins the story "in the beginning."

In Genesis 1, God brings the whole creation into being by speaking the words "Let there be. . . . " Now John connects God's creative speech "in the beginning" with the coming of God here and now. Jesus of Nazareth is not just a prophet who brings God's Word to the people. Jesus *is* God's Word, in the flesh.

It's hard for us to understand how all-encompassing a statement it is that John is making. The Greek word John uses, *Logos*, is more than a reference to a part of speech. *Logos* is the root from which all our "-ology" words come: biology, geology, psychology. Used this way, it describes the academic study of a particular subject. Used more broadly, the related word "logic" refers to a comprehensive system of reasoning. The ancient Greeks used *Logos* as a technical term in the disciplines of philosophy, mathematics, and rhetoric. Depending on its context, *Logos* can be translated not only as "word" but as "speech," "principle," "thought," or "reason." The concept of *Logos* expressed the claim that the universe as a whole had structure and meaning.

So what John is saying here is that the world is not random but was created with a purpose, according to a plan. And that purpose, the meaning of created life, the reason there is something rather than nothing, is God. Philosophy, mathematics, science—these are all tools we can use to help us understand the world and how it works. But the world makes sense because the world was created by God, by a personal God who orders all things for our good.

> *Biblical Wisdom*
> *He is the image of the invisible God, the firstborn of all creation; for in him all things in heaven and on earth were created, things visible and invisible, whether thrones or dominions or rulers or powers—all things have been created through him and for him.*
> Colossians 1:15-16

Theological Thoughts

"As the Word of God, the Logos had spoken in creation, and spoken in the prophets of Israel, and spoken again—and decisively—in the life and teachings of Jesus. As the Reason of God, the Logos made sense out of the madness of the world and the power of evil."[4]

Jaroslav Pelikan

Silence for Meditation

Psalm Fragment
The LORD exists forever;
your word is firmly fixed in heaven.
   Psalm 119:89

Questions to Ponder

- What insights does the word *Logos* offer into the relationship between faith and science?
- How would you explain to someone else the purpose for which the world was created?

Prayer for Today

Help me to recognize your Word, O God, not only in the Scriptures but also in the world you have created. Amen.

Day 3—Friday

. . . and the Word was with God, and the Word was God.
   John 1:1

The doctrine of the Trinity is sometimes referred to as one of the "mysteries of the faith." The belief that God is Father, Son, and Holy Spirit, yet one God, is hard to wrap our heads around. We can't explain it. Try as we might, there are no earthly analogies that accurately communicate the fullness of who the triune God is. We can't explain it, but we believe it.

The word *Trinity* never appears in the New Testament, and even the formula "Father, Son, and Holy Spirit" occurs only a few times. But the doctrine of the Trinity is not a matter of believing "six impossible things before breakfast," as the White Queen tells Alice to do in Lewis Carroll's *Through the Looking Glass*. It results from the struggle of the early church to reconcile its monotheism (belief that there is only one God) with its authentic experience of that God in the person of Jesus and in the coming of the Holy Spirit. Scriptural texts like this one helped Christians to come to an understanding of God as Trinity within unity. This text in particular persuaded the early church that it was not enough to say only that Christians saw three distinct aspects of God. Because the Word was with God "in the beginning," even before the world was created, Trinity is not just how we experience God but names who God is.

The Apostles' Creed and the Nicene Creed, which we still use in worship today, were written by the early church as confessions of faith in the triune God. The word *creed* comes from the Latin word *credo*, which means "I believe." The Creeds didn't—and don't—offer us logical or mathematical explanations. Instead they offer us a personal way to talk about the God in whom we trust.

Martin Luther emphasizes the personal nature of the Apostles' Creed in the Small Catechism. What does our faith in the *triune* God mean? It means that God created *me*. Jesus Christ, God's only Son, has redeemed *me*. The Holy Spirit calls, enlightens, gathers, and sanctifies *me*. These claims are true for all Christians, not just for me; but Luther wants to be sure we hear that they are also true for me, personally.

". . . the Word was with God, and the Word was God." This passage gives us a glimpse of community at the heart of God. In creating the world, God chooses to expand that community to include us.

> *Biblical Wisdom*
> *"On that day you will know that I am in my Father, and you in me, and I in you."*
> John 14:20

Theological Thoughts

"God the Father, light-creator, To Thee laud and honor be.
To Thee, Light of Light begotten, Praise be sung eternally.
Holy Spirit, light-revealer, Glory, glory be to Thee.
Mortals, angels, now and ever Praise the holy Trinity!"[5]

Martin H. Franzmann, ELW 511

Silence for Meditation

Psalm Fragment
Your kingdom is an everlasting kingdom,
and your dominion endures throughout all generations.
The LORD is faithful in all his words,
and gracious in all his deeds.

Psalm 145:13

Questions to Ponder

- Is the concept of mystery a helpful one or is it an obstacle to faith for people today? Is it helpful for you?
- When you pray, do you pray to God the Father? To Jesus? To the Holy Spirit? To the Trinity as a whole?

Prayer for Today

Triune God, as I hear your Word, draw me ever closer into your divine life. Amen.

Day 4—Saturday

Then God said, "Let us make humankind in our image, according to our likeness; and let them have dominion over the fish of the sea, and over the birds of the air, and over the cattle, and over all the wild animals of the earth, and over every creeping thing that creeps upon the earth."

So God created humankind in his image, in the image of God he created them; male and female he created them.
Genesis 1:26-27

What does it mean to be created in the image of God? When I look in the mirror, is what I see really a reflection of God? When I look at my neighbor or my co-worker—or someone I am in conflict with—am I really seeing the image of God?

This is a question that believers have discussed ever since these words were first written. Over time many Christian writers have attempted to define the image of God by identifying the particular human characteristic that most distinguishes humans from God's other creatures. Does the image of God reside in our rationality? In our freedom? In our creativity and capacity for self-transcendence?

Martin Luther approached the question differently. Instead of focusing on a single attribute, Luther described the image of God as being in right relationship with God. Just as a mirror needs something to reflect, humans cannot reveal the image of God when we are separated from the One whom we reflect. Sin distorts the image of God in us because it breaks the relationship God intends for us to share. Christ, the true image of God, restores that relationship.

Being made in the image of God also says something about our relationships with one another, for the God in whose image we are created is three in one. God speaks in the plural in this verse: "Let us make humankind in our image." God also creates in the plural, both men and women. This shows us that all people are made in the image of God. It also shows us that in order to create in God's image at all, God had to make more than one of us!

Now what do you see when you look in the mirror?

Biblical Wisdom
Beloved, we are God's children now; what we will be has not yet been revealed. What we do know is this: when he is revealed, we will be like him, for we will see him as he is.
1 John 3:2

Theological Thoughts

"Therefore my understanding of the image of God is this: that Adam had it in his being and that he not only knew God and believed that He was good, but that he also lived a life that was wholly godly; that is, he was without the fear of death or of any other danger, and was content with God's favor."[6]

Martin Luther

Silence for Meditation

Psalm Fragment
When I look at your heavens, the work of your fingers, the moon and the stars that you have established; what are human beings that you are mindful of them, mortals that you care for them? Yet you have made them a little lower than God, and crowned them with glory and honor.
    Psalm 8:3-5

Questions to Ponder
- Where have you seen the image of God reflected in other people?
- How do others see the image of God when they look at you?

Prayer for Today
Loving God, you made humans in your own image. Help me to live out that image in right relationship with you and with my fellow creatures. Amen.

Day 5—Monday

God blessed them, and God said to them, "Be fruitful and multiply, and fill the earth and subdue it; and have dominion over the fish of the sea and over the birds of the air and over every living thing that moves upon the earth."
    Genesis 1:28

On each day of creation, God calls something new into existence. "Let there be," God says. As a result of God's creative Word, things come into being. And then God calls each of these created things good.

On the sixth day, there's a new twist. God creates humans through the Word, and then God takes things a step further. God doesn't just speak *about* humans. God speaks *to* them, and what God speaks is a word of blessing. God describes a vision for their lives that invites them into a unique relationship with God. God has made the entire created world, but only the human creatures are invited to be stewards of and caretakers for God's creation, working together in God's garden.

Believe it or not, sometimes this passage has been used to justify exploitation of God's good creation for our own benefit. After all, God put us in charge! But dominion is not the same as domination. Does having dominion over the earth mean that everything belongs to us now—or is it a call to be stewards of God's authority? And if we are God's representatives on earth, how are we doing? Air pollution, oil spills, toxic waste—there's plenty of evidence that we're not caring for the created world as well as we could.

Blessing is a frequent theme in the Old Testament. The word "blessed" appears forty times in Genesis alone. One of the things that becomes clear as we read the Scriptures is that God's blessings are meant to be shared. God created the first humans, and now part of God's blessing is for them to continue that creative work. We are blessed in order to be a blessing, working toward the fulfillment that God intends.

Biblical Wisdom

". . . in you all the families of the earth shall be blessed."
Genesis 12:3b

Theological Thoughts

"God no longer wants to act in accordance with His extraordinary or, as the scholastics express it, absolute power but wants to act through His creatures, whom He does not want to be idle. Thus He gives food, not as He did to the Jews in the desert, when He gave manna from heaven, but through labor, when we diligently perform the work of our calling. Furthermore, He no longer wants to form human beings from a clod, as He formed Adam, but He makes use of the union of a male and a female, on whom He bestows His blessing."[7]

Martin Luther

Silence for Meditation

Psalm Fragment
*Bless the L*ORD*, O you his angels,*
you mighty ones who do his bidding,
obedient to his spoken word.
    Psalm 103:20

Questions to Ponder
- How are you doing as a steward of God's creation? What could you do better?
- How is your congregation doing? What could it do better?
- In what other ways can you live as God's blessing for others?

Prayer for Today
Continue to bless me, Lord, so that I may be an instrument of your blessing to the world you have made. Amen.

Day 6—Tuesday

Then God said, "Let there be. . . ."
    Genesis 1:3-31

A good cook doesn't always need a recipe. Once you have mastered the basics of cooking, you can improvise—often with delightful results.

The first chapter of Genesis portrays God as a master chef. God uses the same basic recipe—"Let there be"—and then improvises. Let there be: light, day and night, sky, land and seas, vegetation, sun, moon, and stars, fish and birds, animals, and finally, people. God's recipe is simple: no slicing and dicing, no mixing and baking. God's Word simply creates what it names. And before these six days God made this decision: Let there be something rather than nothing!

Twentieth-century Lutheran theologian Paul Tillich describes God as the power of being in all that is. His point, I think, is that the "let there be" continues. Everything there exists not simply because God said so "in the beginning," but because God continues to say so, sustaining the creation day after day. Perhaps we could imagine the world as a balloon that remains inflated because it continues to be filled and refilled with God's breath.

The wonderful hymn "Earth and All Stars" by Herb Brokering demonstrates this point beautifully. The first stanza names things we recognize as part of the created world: earth, stars, wind, and rain. But the later stanzas name things that are clearly the work of human effort: musical instruments, engines and steel, classrooms and labs, and more. These are things made by God's human creatures, but they are called upon to praise God along with the rest of creation. All these things exist because of God's creative power, whether God called them into existence "in the beginning" or whether they were made by those whom God entrusted with continuing the work of creation. God has given us a recipe for life—Let there be!—and the freedom to improvise God's new song.

> *Biblical Wisdom*
> *"But now thus says the Lord, he who created you, O Jacob, he who formed you, O Israel: Do not fear, for I have redeemed you; I have called you by name, you are mine."*
> Isaiah 43:1

> *Theological Thoughts*

"That which is created by the Word out of nothing, that which is called forth into being, remains sustained by the sight of God. . . . God sees that it is good and his eye resting upon the work preserves the work in being. Therefore the world is preserved only by the one who is its Creator and alone for the one who is its Creator. The world is preserved not for its own sake but for the sake of the sight of God."[8]

Dietrich Bonhoeffer

Silence for Meditation

Psalm Fragment
Let everything that breathes praise the LORD!
Praise the LORD!
  Psalm 150:6

Questions to Ponder
- Do you think of yourself as a creative person? What gifts has God given you to use in the world?
- Who is responsible for the harmful things that have been created?

More Questions to Ponder
This is the end of the first week of your Lenten journey with the Word. As you reflect back on the week, what themes do you notice? When in the past week have you most clearly felt God's presence?

Prayer for Today
Ever-creating God, let there be a new day today, full of possibilities to celebrate your goodness. Amen.

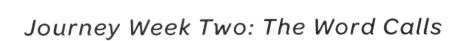

Journey Week Two: The Word Calls

Day 7

> *In the second year of King Darius, in the sixth month, on the first day of the month, the word of the Lord came by the prophet Haggai to Zerubbabel son of Shealtiel, governor of Judah, and to Joshua son of Jehozadak, the high priest.*
>
> Haggai 1:1

Days 8–9

> *Now the word of the Lord came to me saying, "Before I formed you in the womb I knew you, and before you were born I consecrated you; I appointed you a prophet to the nations."*
>
> *Then I said, "Ah, Lord God! Truly I do not know how to speak, for I am only a boy."*
>
> Jeremiah 1:4-6

Day 10

*Now the L*ORD *came and stood there, calling as before, "Samuel! Samuel!"
And Samuel said, "Speak, for your servant is listening."*
   1 Samuel 3:10

Day 11

*After this he went out and saw a tax collector named Levi, sitting at the
tax booth; and he said to him, "Follow me." And he got up, left everything,
and followed him.*
   Luke 5:27-28

Day 12

*Then he said to them all, "If any want to become my followers, let them
deny themselves and take up their cross daily and follow me. For those
who want to save their life will lose it, and those who lose their life for my
sake will save it. What does it profit them if they gain the whole world, but
lose or forfeit themselves?*
   Luke 9:23-25

Day 7—Wednesday

> *In the second year of King Darius, in the sixth month, on the first day of the month, the word of the Lord came by the prophet Haggai to Zerubbabel son of Shealtiel, governor of Judah, and to Joshua son of Jehozadak, the high priest.*
>
> Haggai 1:1

Not the most exciting text, is it? To be honest, I don't spend a lot of time reading the book of Haggai. But the details that seem least interesting point us to what's really most important about this text: its specificity. The prophet names particular people, places, and times, so that his hearers know he's talking about something that really happened, something they can relate to the particularities of their own lives. God's word is not generic. It speaks to real people in the particular "here and now" they inhabit.

This is also the reason for those genealogies that sometimes bog us down when we read the Scriptures. To us, they're long lists of names, hard to pronounce and not very interesting. But the first hearers and readers of the Word recognized these names. We might say that they make up the family tree of faith.

Being faithful to the Scriptures does not mean we need to master ancient history, learning all the names and dates and stories. Learning more about the Scriptures can certainly enrich our faith life. But faithfulness is more about letting the Word of God shape our lives than about acquiring biblical knowledge. The Scriptures offer us a Word from God that is both timeless and timely, both historical and personal. When you encounter unfamiliar names and places in the Scriptures, don't just learn more about the history. Think about how you can connect the stories of past believers to your own life today. Let the Word of the Lord come to you in this year, in this month, on this day.

Biblical Wisdom
Long ago God spoke to our ancestors in many and various ways by the prophets, but in these last days he has spoken to us by a Son, whom he appointed heir of all things, through whom he also created the worlds.
Hebrews 1:1-2

Theological Thoughts

"The history to which we point when we speak of revelation is not the succession of events which an uninterested spectator can see from the outside but our own history. It is one thing to perceive from a safe distance the occurrences in a stranger's life and quite a different thing to ponder the path of one's own destiny, to deal with the why and whence and whither of one's own existence."[9]

H. Richard Niebuhr

Silence for Meditation

Psalm Fragment
O Israel, hope in the LORD from this time on and forevermore.
  Psalm 131:3

Questions to Ponder
- Haggai was given a message from God for the local governor and for the high priest. What do you think about that? Is it relevant to questions about the relationship between church and state today?
- How do you think political and economic contexts shape the way people hear God's word in their lives today?
- How would you describe our "here and now" to others? What Word of God might the world need to hear today?

Prayer for Today

God, you are the Alpha and the Omega, the beginning and the end. Speak to me also in the present hour. Amen.

Day 8—Thursday

Now the word of the LORD came to me saying, "Before I formed you in the womb I knew you, and before you were born I consecrated you; I appointed you a prophet to the nations."
  Jeremiah 1:4-5

In the baby books we kept for our children, there was a page to record our hopes for them. My husband and I had a hard time deciding what to write on that page. We didn't want to be pushy parents who force their own agendas on their children. I guess we just wanted our children to be themselves, whoever that turned out to be. Of course, we wanted them to be healthy and happy. We wanted them to grow as faithful Christians. But beyond that, we were comfortable letting the details unfold along the way.

How do things look from God's perspective? God has clear expectations for Jeremiah. God tells Jeremiah exactly what he will become: a prophet who will speak God's Word to the nations. Christians who are trying to discern whether God has a specific plan for their lives might be envious of this clarity, but Jeremiah himself seems rather unhappy about what God expects him to do.

I wonder, though, if there's a sense in which God's plan for Jeremiah is the same plan God has for all of us. We may not have dramatic stories in which we hear a personal message from God. But surely God says of each one of us, "Before I formed you in the womb I knew you." In baptism every Christian receives the same blessing and the same calling as Jeremiah: claimed by God, we are commissioned to share God's Word with others. True, most of us aren't given instructions as specific as those God gives to Jeremiah, but the basic plan is the same. The details just unfold as we go along.

God's call continues to work itself out throughout our lives. Perhaps you've seen the bumper sticker that says, "Please be patient. God isn't finished with me yet." I wonder if it might be even more accurate to say, "Please be patient. God's work with me has only just begun!"

Biblical Wisdom
For surely I know the plans I have for you, says the Lord, plans for your welfare and not for harm, to give you a future with hope.
Jeremiah 29:11

Theological Thoughts
"If you are seeking after God, you may be sure of this: God is seeking you much more. He is the Lover, and you are his beloved. He has promised himself to you. . . . I tell you again—it is not of your own doing at all, this moment when

your soul awakens. He creates in you the desire to find him and run after him—
to follow wherever he leads you, and to press peacefully against his heart wherever he is."[10]

St. John of the Cross

Silence for Meditation

Psalm Fragment
For it was you who formed my inward parts;
You knit me together in my mother's womb.
I praise you, for I am fearfully and wonderfully made.
Wonderful are your works;
that I know very well.
  Psalm 139:13-14

Questions to Ponder
- What expectations do others have for you? What expectations do you have
  for yourself? What do you think God expects from your life? How similar or
  different are these expectations?
- When did you first become aware that God loves you and wants the best for
  your life?

Prayer for Today
God of the prophets, help me to hear your Word with clarity and to speak your
Word with conviction. Amen.

Day 9—Friday

Now the word of the LORD came to me . . . Then I said, "Ah, Lord GOD! Truly I
do not know how to speak, for I am only a boy."
  Jeremiah 1:4, 6

So many of God's messengers start out full of excuses. Moses says he doesn't speak well. Jonah doesn't think the people of Nineveh deserve a chance at God's mercy. Jeremiah says he's too young.

When Moses said he couldn't speak well, God told him to take his brother Aaron with him. When Jonah ran the other way, God sent a whale to spit him back in the right direction. However unqualified we feel, God provides what we need to do the work God has called us to do.

Jeremiah's excuse is one we tend to apply to others as well as to ourselves. Sometimes we make excuses to cover our own sense of inadequacy. But sometimes we judge others on the basis of how they appear to us. Would God really choose a messenger so young? Or so old? Would God really choose to speak through a poor, uneducated person, or a person of a different ethnicity or cultural background? How easy it is for us to dismiss people because they don't measure up to our expectations.

People looked at Jesus that way too. They asked, Is this not the carpenter's son from Nazareth? We know his mother and his brothers. How could he possibly have a message from God? Surely God would choose someone more appropriate than this!

But the God who calls unexpected messengers also equips them for their work. And in the fullness of time, God chose to become the Messenger as well as the Message.

Biblical Wisdom

Consider your own call, brothers and sisters: not many of you were wise by human standards, not many were powerful, not many were of noble birth. But God chose what is foolish in the world to shame the wise; God chose what is weak in the world to shame the strong.

1 Corinthians 1:26-27

Theological Thoughts

"But this I say for myself, I am also a doctor and a preacher, just as learned and experienced as all of them who are so high and mighty. Nevertheless, each morning, and whenever else I have time, I do as a child who is being taught the catechism and I read and recite word for word the Lord's Prayer, the Ten

Commandments, the Creed, the Psalms, etc. I must still read and study the catechism daily, and yet I cannot master it as I wish, but must remain a child and pupil of the catechism, and I also do so gladly."[11]

Martin Luther

Silence for Meditation

Psalm Fragment
Even before a word is on my tongue,
O Lord, you know it completely.
  Psalm 139:4

Questions to Ponder
- What excuses have you made to keep you from responding to God's call?
- How easy or hard is it for you to hear God's call through others?
- How do your congregation and community use the gifts of younger people and of older people?

Prayer for Today
God, open my eyes and ears to receive the messengers you send to me, and open my mouth to be the messenger you call me to be. Amen.

Day 10—Saturday

Now the Lord came and stood there, calling as before, "Samuel! Samuel!"
And Samuel said, "Speak, for your servant is listening."
  1 Samuel 3:10

I can identify with Samuel. God calls Samuel over and over again, and Samuel keeps misunderstanding. He hears a voice but concludes that it is his mentor, the priest Eli, who is calling him. So Samuel dutifully reports to Eli, who sends him back to bed.

In the movie *Field of Dreams*, Kevin Costner's character, Ray Kinsella, tells his wife, Annie, that he has heard a voice in the cornfield telling him, "If you build it, he will come." His wife asks, "If you build what, who will come?" It takes Ray the rest of the movie to figure out the real answer to that question. It's not just about Shoeless Joe Jackson coming back to life to play ball again. It's not just about "easing the pain" of former writer and activist Terence Mann. The real reason the persistent voice calls to Ray is to bring about reconciliation between Ray and his father. But to figure that out, Ray has to take one step at a time on a cross-country journey.

Samuel, too, has to learn how to listen for the real meaning of the voice that keeps calling him, the message behind the message. He thinks Eli is calling, which isn't the case. But Eli's role in the story is indispensable. Eli keeps turning Samuel back to bed, to the place where he has heard the call and where it is likely to come again. And as Eli figures out what's really going on, he is able to give Samuel the advice he needs to respond to God's call the next time it comes.

God often does speak to us through others. But it's still a challenge to learn how to listen. When are we hearing what God is really saying to us, and when are we hearing what we want to hear? It's a lifelong journey and one best undertaken with faithful companions.

Biblical Wisdom
Then afterward
I will pour out my spirit on all flesh;
your sons and your daughters shall prophesy,
your old men shall dream dreams,
and your young men shall see visions.
* Joel 2:28*

Theological Thoughts
"For in truth we are not called once only, but many times; all through our life Christ is calling us. He called us first in Baptism; but afterwards also; whether we obey His voice or not, He graciously calls us still. If we fall from our Baptism He calls us to repent; if we are striving to fulfill our calling, he calls us on from grace to grace, and from holiness to holiness, while life is given us. . . ."[12]
John Henry Newman

Silence for Meditation

Psalm Fragment
I rise before dawn and cry for help;
I put my hope in your words.
    Psalm 119:147

Questions to Ponder

- How have you heard God's call in your life? Who has helped you hear and respond to God's call?
- Do you think God calls everyone? Why or why not?

Prayer for Today
Help me to say with Samuel, "Speak, for your servant is listening." Help me to say with Mary, "Here am I, the servant of the Lord; let it be with me according to your word." Amen.

Day 11—Monday

After this he went out and saw a tax collector named Levi, sitting at the tax booth; and he said to him, "Follow me." And he got up, left everything, and followed him.
    Luke 5:27-28

Luke makes it sound so simple. The tax collector didn't take the time to write out pro and con lists. It was drop everything and "just do it." What was it about Jesus that prompted such an immediate and total response? Was it really that easy? Could I do the same thing?

Luke also tells us about an encounter between Jesus and another tax collector, Zacchaeus (Luke 19). For Zacchaeus, following Jesus wasn't a matter of leaving his work behind. It was a matter of making restitution for the money he'd taken from others. And yet Zacchaeus seemed to do it joyfully and without hesitation, paying back even more than he had taken.

We, on the other hand, seem to struggle with keeping our New Year's resolutions or giving up things for Lent. Let's not even think about what it would take to change our whole way of life! Old habits and comfortable lifestyles are hard to give up.

Of course, Jesus encountered other would-be disciples who chose not to follow. The rich young man decided not to sell all he had and give to the poor in order to follow Jesus. Others chose to tend to the harvest or their family obligations rather than joining Jesus on his journey without an opportunity to first tie up loose ends. The call to follow seemed too big, too all-encompassing.

The motto of twelve-step programs like Alcoholics Anonymous is "One day at a time." Maybe there's a message for disciples and would-be disciples in that. Changing my whole life seems too overwhelming to contemplate. But just as the alcoholic can say, "I will not have a drink today," so I can follow Jesus today, one day at a time, one step at a time. Tomorrow will be another day, another opportunity to continue on the journey.

Biblical Wisdom

"He calls his own sheep by name and leads them out. When he has brought out all his own, he goes ahead of them, and the sheep follow him because they know his voice."

John 10:3b-4

Theological Thoughts

"When Levi was called from the receipt of custom and Peter from his nets, there was no doubt that Jesus meant business. Both of them were to leave everything and follow. . . . Only one thing was required in each case—to rely on Christ's word, and cling to it as offering greater security than all the securities in the world."[13]

Dietrich Bonhoeffer

Silence for Meditation

Psalm Fragment
I rejoice at your word
like one who finds great spoil.
Psalm 119:162

Questions to Ponder

- Have you had to give up anything to follow Jesus?
- Do you think it's harder to be a Christian in some occupations than in others? Why or why not?
- Are there similarities between a Christian going to church and an alcoholic or addict going to an Alcoholics Anonymous or another twelve-step meeting?

Prayer for Today

Lord Jesus, reorder my priorities and transform my life so that I may follow you when you call. Amen.

Day 12—Tuesday

Then he said to them all, "If any want to become my followers, let them deny themselves and take up their cross daily and follow me."
Luke 9:23

Yesterday's text described Levi leaving everything behind to become one of Jesus' disciples. Today's text shows us the other side of the coin. Following Jesus is not just about what we leave behind but about what we take on: the cross.

One of the ancient Lenten disciplines is giving up something for Lent. This tradition comes to us from the observance of the Jewish Passover, when the use of leaven is prohibited in memory of the first Passover. If you've experienced the tradition of a Shrove Tuesday pancake breakfast or supper, that's a related tradition for Christians: making pancakes was a good way to use up butter, eggs, and yeast before the Lenten period of fasting began on Ash Wednesday.

Some Christians still give up things for Lent: chocolate, caffeine, television. But today many Christians prefer to think instead about taking something on.

Even fasting or abstaining can be reinterpreted, seen differently: I'm not giving up television and movies, I'm making more time for daily devotions.

In *The Cost of Discipleship*, Dietrich Bonhoeffer wrote, "When Christ calls a man, he bids him come and die."[14] But Christ himself goes before us on this journey to the cross. Christ goes before us to the grave, and Christ is raised to new life as the first fruits of the resurrection that he promises to also share with us.

It's common for people to describe a difficult personal situation as being someone's "cross to bear." The late Swedish Lutheran bishop Krister Stendahl was once heard to challenge that pious sentiment by insisting, "A cross is something you choose!" Jesus freely chose to carry the cross for our sake. Because Jesus chose to bear our burdens, we are freed to bear the burdens of others.

Biblical Wisdom
Bear one another's burdens, and in this way you will fulfill the law of Christ.
Galatians 6:2

Theological Thoughts
"As followers of Jesus Christ, we are not to save death and dying for the end of our lives. Life in Christ requires dying now. Those who hope in God as the redeemer from death must enter into the vulnerable, suffering love that leads to the cross. The entire Christian life draws us into an ongoing 'death,' in which we die to everything that thwarts God's intentions for life, peace, and joy."[15]
Amy Plantinga Pauw

Silence for Meditation

Psalm Fragment
I am severely afflicted;
give me life, O Lord, according to your word.
Psalm 119:107

Questions to Ponder

- Have you given up anything for Lent or taken on any new spiritual disciplines?
- Look around you. Where—in your family, in your community, in the world—are there burdens that you could help to carry for others?
- What difference does it make whether we think of carrying the cross and following Jesus as an individual or a communal enterprise?

More Questions to Ponder

This is the end of the second week of your Lenten journey with the Word. As you reflect back on the week, what themes do you notice? When in the past week have you most clearly felt God's presence?

Prayer for Today

Lord Jesus, give me the courage and the strength to take up your cross for the sake of others. Amen.

Journey Week Three: The Word Commands

Days 13–18

Then God spoke all these words:

I am the L<small>ORD</small> your God, who brought you out of the land of Egypt, out of the house of slavery; you shall have no other gods before me.

You shall not make for yourself an idol, whether in the form of anything that is in heaven above, or that is on the earth beneath, or that is in the water under the earth. You shall not bow down to them or worship them; for I the L<small>ORD</small> your God am a jealous God, punishing children for the iniquity of parents, to the third and the fourth generation of those who reject me, but showing steadfast love to the thousandth generation of those who love me and keep my commandments.

You shall not make wrongful use of the name of the L<small>ORD</small> your God, for the L<small>ORD</small> will not acquit anyone who misuses his name.

Remember the sabbath day, and keep it holy. Six days you shall labor and do all your work. But the seventh day is a sabbath to the Lord your God; you shall not do any work—you, your son or your daughter, your male or female slave, your livestock, or the alien resident in your towns. For in six days the Lord made heaven and earth, the sea, and all that is in them, but rested the seventh day; therefore the Lord blessed the sabbath day and consecrated it.

Honor your father and your mother, so that your days may be long in the land that the Lord your God is giving you.

You shall not murder.

You shall not commit adultery.

You shall not steal.

You shall not bear false witness against your neighbor.

You shall not covet your neighbor's house; you shall not covet your neighbor's wife, or male or female slave, or ox, or donkey, or anything that belongs to your neighbor.
    Exodus 20:1-17

Day 13—Wednesday

Then God spoke all these words.
Exodus 20:1

The Ten Commandments are recorded twice in the Scriptures, here in Exodus 20 and also in Deuteronomy 5. When we read the Exodus text, we may be surprised by what it doesn't say. Neither the number "ten" nor the word "commandments" appears in the text. What follows are called "words," not "commandments."

Like the Greek word *logos*, the Hebrew word *dabhar* conveys a meaning deeper than just a vocabulary term. It can refer to a thing or an event as well as a word. For instance, the Hebrew phrase which we would translate literally "words of the day" actually means events of the day. Words, especially God's words, have the power to make things happen. What makes these particular words commandments for us is not their content or their form ("do this, don't do that"), but their source. Because these are words from God, not from someone else, they have authority in the lives of God's people.

It's easy for us to rush past the simple word *then* in this verse, but it's not just a filler word. *Then* always implies a *before*. So what happens before this? God summons Moses to come up to Mount Sinai. And before that? Well, it's been a long journey. God hears the cries of the Hebrew slaves in Egypt, sends Moses to challenge Pharaoh for their release, and leads them safely across the Red Sea. In short, these words are spoken in the context of an ongoing relationship, a relationship in which God has already shown faithfulness to the people. And so, before the words of command come, God reminds the people of this relationship.

Perhaps you've heard the comedian's line about the parent who threatens the misbehaving child by saying, "I brought you into this world, and I can take you out of it!" Perhaps you've seen the T-shirt that says, "Because I'm the Mom. That's why!" That's not the kind of authority God exercises. God's authority is expressed as love rather than raw power: "I am the God who created you. I am the God who redeems you. Here are the words of life which I give to you. Listen."

Biblical Wisdom

"I will take you as my people, and I will be your God. You shall know that I am the Lord your God, who has freed you from the burdens of the Egyptians."

   Exodus 6:7

Theological Thoughts

"The Christian story does not provide a special set of moral guidelines. Justice is justice, peace is peace, food is food, and God lets rain fall on the unjust as well as the just. At the same time, the Christian story gives a special meaning to human activity, a special motive for doing good. It is a story of resurrection and new life, and Christians receive staying power from this."[16]

   Martin E. Marty

Silence for Meditation

Psalm Fragment

He is mindful of his covenant forever,
of the word that he commanded, for a thousand generations.
   Psalm 105:8

Questions to Ponder

- How does thinking about the Ten Commandments as part of an ongoing conversation with God, rather than as laws to be obeyed, change the way you see them?
- What are the consequences of not keeping God's Commandments?
- What kind of authority do you have in your workplace, in your family, and in your community?

Prayer for Today

Faithful God, help me to hear your word and to follow it. Amen.

Day 14—Thursday

> *I am the L ORD your God, who brought you out of the land of Egypt, out of the house of slavery.*
> Exodus 20:2

When Moses asked for God's name earlier in the book of Exodus, God responded, "I am who I am." This wasn't a particularly satisfying answer for Moses, and it's not particularly satisfying for us, either. In fact, it sounds like an answer intended to end the conversation.

In this text God provides a much more specific self-identification: "I am the L ORD your God, who brought you out of the land of Egypt, out of the house of slavery." Why the difference? Why not give this answer earlier in the story? I think the reason is that Moses and the people now, on this side of Egypt, finally have a context to understand who God is. They couldn't have understood who God is before they'd experienced what God did for them.

It's human nature to resist being told what to do. We like to be the ones who give commands, not the ones who get them. The people of Israel had just been rescued from slavery in Egypt, and now they're being given a new set of instructions. The Ten Commandments are given to newly liberated slaves—from the one who liberated them. The people must have asked themselves if they were just trading one taskmaster, Pharaoh, for another, God. That's why it's so important for God to remind the people of the relationship they have—a relationship of care, not simply a relationship of power.

Computer commands may be a good analogy to help us think about this. We push certain buttons and combine certain keystrokes, not to exercise power over the computer but because doing so will help us use the computer to accomplish our tasks. Some of these commands we figure out by trial and error, but we can also turn to a hardware or software manual for valuable instruction. Likewise, God's commands are not arbitrary. God is not interested in demonstrating power over us; God is committed to our welfare and to providing us with the knowledge that will help us live life in accordance with our Creator's loving intentions for us. The end of the story is not "I am who I am," but "I am for you!"

Biblical Wisdom

"I do not call you servants any longer, because the servant does not know what the master is doing; but I have called you friends, because I have made known to you everything that I have heard from my Father."
    John 15:15

Theological Thoughts

"A Christian is a perfectly free lord of all, subject to none. A Christian is a perfectly dutiful servant of all, subject to all."[17]

Martin Luther

Silence for Meditation

Psalm Fragment

You have dealt well with your servant,
O Lord, according to your word.
    Psalm 119:65

Questions to Ponder

· How have you experienced God's liberating power in your life?
· Where in our world today is there need for liberation? How can God's people be witnesses to and agents of this liberation?

Prayer for Today

Liberating God, continue to liberate me from bondage to everything that opposes you. Amen.

Day 15—Friday

You shall have no other gods before me.
    Exodus 20:3

The First Commandment is an easy one for us to take for granted. Perhaps it applied to Old Testament believers who lived in a world where different groups of people believed in different gods, but this isn't a problem for us. Or is it?

Martin Luther explains each of the Ten Commandments in his Small Catechism. The meaning of the First Commandment, according to Luther, is that "We should fear, love, and trust in God above all things." But this is easier said than done. In his Large Catechism, Luther offers additional insight. He defines a god as whatever we put our trust in. Maybe it's money, or power, or some other form of success. Maybe it's even me—trusting in my own ability to take charge of my life and to provide for those I love. Luther's insight shows how relevant this commandment still is for us. The God we confess our faith in on Sunday may not be our "working god," what we really depend on as we live out our daily lives. I once saw a church sign that expressed the point this way: "A self-made man always worships his creator."

Alcoholics Anonymous and other twelve-step programs have the same insight. They talk about faith in "a Power greater than ourselves" and about turning one's life over "to the care of God as we understand Him." This open-ended description of faith as trust makes sense for an organization that serves people with many different belief systems. As Christians, however, we have a very specific understanding of who God is. Christian faith is not about how strongly or sincerely someone believes. Christian faith is about putting our trust in the God whose trustworthiness has been proven time and again: the God who created the world, the God who called Abraham, Isaac, and Jacob, the God who freed Israel from slavery, the God who raised Jesus from the dead. No other "god" is worthy of our trust, because no other god has done so much for us. No other "god" is worthy of our trust, because no other god has truly gone to hell and back to deliver us from sin and death.

Biblical Wisdom
"There is salvation in no one else, for there is no other name under heaven given among mortals by which we must be saved."
Acts 4:12

Theological Thoughts

"A 'god' is the term for that to which we are to look for all good and in which we are to find refuge in all need. Therefore, to have a god is nothing else than to trust and believe in that one with your whole heart. As I have often said, it is the trust and faith of the heart alone that make both God and an idol. If your faith and trust are right, then your God is the true one. Conversely, where your trust is false and wrong, there you do not have the true God. For these two belong together, faith and God. Anything on which your heart relies and depends, I say, that is really your God."[18]

Martin Luther

Silence for Meditation

Psalm Fragment
In God, whose word I praise,
in God I trust; I am not afraid.
    Psalm 56:4

Questions to Ponder

· What are you tempted to put first in your life? How do you refocus your priorities?
· How do you know God is trustworthy? How can you communicate God's trustworthiness to others?

Prayer for Today

Faithful God, as I live each day, help me to grow in my trust of you. Amen.

Day 16—Saturday

Remember the sabbath day, and keep it holy.
    Exodus 20:8

This is one of my favorite commandments—and one of the strangest ones. How odd it seems that we should need to be commanded to observe the Sabbath—in other words, commanded to rest! Or is it? In our fast-paced world, are weekends really a time of rest for us anymore, or are they the time filled by the tasks and errands we didn't have time to get done during the workweek? Remember when advertisers used to pitch their new products as "labor-saving devices"? New technologies do save us time and effort, but they also make it possible for us to work nonstop, checking e-mails on vacation, fielding text messages at a restaurant.

But the sabbath is about more than just unscheduled time. We are not commanded to rest simply for rest's sake, but for the sake of remembrance. As God rested from the work of creation on the seventh day, so we creatures made in God's image should also rest from our labors. In the Old and New Testaments, the word *remember* means more than just thinking about the past. To remember has the sense of making the past come alive again in the present moment. When we remember the sabbath this way, we find ourselves resting in the presence of God.

Faithful Jews observe the sabbath on Saturday, the seventh day of the week. Seventh Day Adventists are Christians who continue to observe the sabbath on Saturday, but most Christians consider Sunday to be the new sabbath. Why the shift from Saturday to Sunday? Because the day on which God rested from the work of creation has been surpassed in significance by the day on which God raised Jesus from the dead.

This rhythm is built into the church's Lenten observance too. We do not count Sundays in the forty days of Lent. Even in the midst of this time of repentance and waiting, we have a weekly reminder—and celebration—of the good news of Easter.

> *Biblical Wisdom*
> *"Come to me, all you that are weary and are carrying heavy burdens, and I will give you rest. Take my yoke upon you, and learn from me; for I am gentle and humble in heart, and you will find rest for your souls. For my yoke is easy, and my burden is light."*
> Matthew 11:28-30

Theological Thoughts

"The Exodus commandment to 'remember' the Sabbath day is grounded in the story of creation. . . . In both work and rest, human beings are in the image of God. . . . In Deuteronomy, the commandment to 'observe' the Sabbath day is tied to the experience of a people newly released from bondage. Slaves cannot take a day off; free people can."[19]

Dorothy Bass

Silence for Meditation

Psalm Fragment
I bow down toward your holy temple
and give thanks to your name for your steadfast love and your faithful-ness;
for you have exalted your name and your word
above everything.
    Psalm 138:2

Questions to Ponder
· How do you make sabbath time in your life? Is this different at different times and circumstances of your life?
· How can pastors and others with Sunday responsibilities make sabbath time?
· If our culture took sabbath seriously, what would change?
· How would you respond to someone who says, "I can worship God on the golf course on Sunday just as well as if I were in church"?

Prayer for Today

You made us for yourself and our hearts find no peace until they rest in you.[20] Amen.

St. Augustine

Day 17—Monday

You shall not. . . .
Exodus 20:4, 5, 7, 10, 13, 14, 15, 16, 17

What a long list of prohibitions! But not as long as it could be! In the Jewish understanding of the Torah (God's Law), there are 613 commandments, equally binding on faithful Jews. What we call the Ten Commandments are understood by Jews as general categories into which all 613 commandments can be sorted.

Some days the *don'ts* in our lives are overwhelming. I remember as a young mother being told not to say "don't" too much to toddlers. Especially for children at an early stage of language acquisition, it's better to name the desired behavior than the forbidden one. "Stay in the yard" is easier for a young child to understand than "Don't go in the street." In fact, "Don't do x, y, or z" might actually give a toddler new ideas for inappropriate behavior.

So it's not as simple as "Just say no." Nor is it as simple as saying, "Just do it." In 1518, in a debate called the Heidelberg Disputation, Martin Luther made the point this way: "The law says, 'do this,' and it is never done. Grace says, 'believe in this,' and everything is already done."[21] If we approach life as a lengthy to-do list, we're bound to come up short. Luther suggests a dramatically different approach. Instead of focusing on our own behavior, on our own obedience, the place to center our Christian life is in what God in Christ has already done for us!

The Commandments were spoken to the people of Israel after God had freed them from slavery in Egypt. It's God's gracious act of loving rescue that should inspire the people to respond, to live a life worthy of the freedom they have been given. How much more powerful an experience of God's love and grace Christians have in the life, death, and resurrection of Jesus! Faith in God's promise to forgive our sin for Jesus' sake frees us from keeping score and frees us to live in response to God's grace. It doesn't get much better than that!

Biblical Wisdom
What then are we to say? Should we continue in sin in order that grace may abound? By no means! How can we who died to sin go on living in it?
Romans 6:1-2

Theological Thoughts

"This life, therefore, is not godliness but the process of becoming godly, not health but getting well, not being but becoming, not rest but exercise. We are not now what we shall be, but we are on the way. The process is not yet finished, but it is actively going on. This is not the goal but it is the right road. At present, everything does not gleam and sparkle, but everything is being cleansed."[22]

Martin Luther

Silence for Meditation

Psalm Fragment
I treasure your word in my heart,
so that I may not sin against you.
　　Psalm 119:11

Questions to Ponder
- How would you explain the Christian life to someone else, without using any "don'ts"?
- What does "dying to sin" mean for you?

Prayer for Today
Giver of every good, may your words dwell within my heart and bear fruit in my life. Amen.

Day 18—Tuesday

Six days you shall labor and do all your work.
　　Exodus 20:9

It's easy to overlook this little verse. We don't count it as one of the Commandments; it's just an explanation of the command to observe the sabbath. But I like this little verse because it shifts our focus from the "shall nots" to the "shalls." It some ways, it's easier to come up with a list of prohibitions: Don't do this, and don't do that, and you'll be fine. But what *should* we do?!

When Martin Luther explains the Ten Commandments in the Small Catechism, he gives each one a positive meaning as well as a negative one. We might say he shifts the focus from "the letter of the law" to "the spirit of the law." Not committing adultery is a goal that many of us manage to achieve without much difficulty. But how about helping our neighbors to strengthen their own marriages and helping our young people to understand sex as a God-given gift rather than recreation? Most of us aren't put in situations where we've been faced with killing someone, but we have harmed people through our words and actions, and we certainly haven't done everything we could to eliminate such life-threatening conditions as poverty, hunger, disease, and war.

Luther used the concept of vocation to convey his understanding of what it means to live the Christian life. In a time when the word *vocation* was typically limited to priests, monks, and nuns, Luther encouraged all Christians to consider the roles and responsibilities in their own lives as vocations, as worthy callings from God. Being faithful in the regular work of one's life—on the job, in the home, and in the community—mattered to God. Luther used the Ten Commandments less as a list of rules than as a window for seeing ways in which to help and serve our neighbors.

We don't need to try to impress God with how religious or how righteous (self-righteous!) we are. God gives us more than enough to do, simply by placing us in the lives we are in. God gives us bodies to use. God gives us neighbors to serve. And God blesses the work we do in the world God has made.

Biblical Wisdom
Whatever your hand finds to do, do with your might.
Ecclesiastes 9:10a

Theological Thoughts
"Thus the prayer of the Christian reaches beyond its set time and extends into the heart of his work. It includes the whole day, and in doing so, it does not hinder the work; it promotes it, affirms it, and lends it meaning and joy. Thus every word, every work, every labor of the Christian becomes a prayer."[23]
Dietrich Bonhoeffer

Silence for Meditation

Psalm Fragment
The sum of your word is truth;
and every one of your righteous ordinances endures forever.
    Psalm 119:160

Questions to Ponder
- Is being a Christian more about what you do or about what you don't do?
- How do you relate your work, whether paid or unpaid, to your faith?
- Does the "time and talent" list in your congregation include opportunities for service that take place outside the church building?

More Questions to Ponder
This is the end of the third week of your Lenten journey with the Word. As you reflect back on the week, what themes do you notice? When in the past week have you most clearly felt God's presence?

Prayer for Today
Help us to provide worthy work and fair compensation for all people. Amen.

Journey Week Four: The Word Saves

Days 19–24

*In the beginning was the Word, and the Word was with God, and the
Word was God. He was in the beginning with God. All things came into
being through him, and without him not one thing came into being. What
has come into being in him was life, and the life was the light of all people.
The light shines in the darkness, and the darkness did not overcome it.*

*. . . He was in the world, and the world came into being through him; yet
the world did not know him. He came to what was his own, and his own
people did not accept him. But to all who received him, who believed in
his name, he gave power to become children of God, who were born, not
of blood or of the will of the flesh or of the will of man, but of God.*

*And the Word became flesh and lived among us, and we have seen his
glory, the glory as of a father's only son, full of grace and truth.*
    John 1:1-5, 10-14

Day 19—Wednesday

In the beginning was the Word, and the Word was with God, and the
Word was God.
John 1:1

We've encountered this text before, but we are no longer "in the beginning."
We're almost halfway through our Lenten journey. We have spent time reflecting
on how the Word creates, calls, and commands. Now we consider how the Word
saves.

John 1:1 takes us back to the beginning, the creation. But then John brings
us forward to the second act, the second half of Lent, to the future. The Word
through whom creation comes to life is the Word through whom creation is
restored. This Word spoken at the beginning of time now takes on human form
and enters into history in person.

An early Christian bishop, Irenaeus of Lyons, speculated that the incarnation would have happened even if humans had never sinned. Irenaeus thought
that God's creative vision and action would eventually culminate in God entering
into the creation personally. But of course human sin provided an added reason
for the incarnation. The Word became flesh not only to enter into the creation,
but to save it.

It won't surprise you to learn that I wrote this devotional book on a computer, using word processing software. One of the features I appreciate is the
automatic prompt that won't allow me to close a document without asking, "Do
you want to save the changes you have made?" Of course, saving files is a practi-
cal thing to do. When changes are made—changes for the better—we want to
preserve them. Saving isn't just about keeping, but about improving. Can you
imagine John 1 in light of word processing software—God the Word responding
to the prompt, "Do you want to save the changes you have made to your creation?" God's answer is a resounding "Yes!"

Biblical Wisdom
But when the fullness of time had come, God sent his Son, born of a woman, born under the law, in order to redeem those who were under the law, so that we might receive adoption as children.
   Galatians 4:4-5

Theological Thoughts
"I know that the Immovable comes down; I know that the invisible appears to me; I know that he who is far outside the whole creation takes me within himself and hides me in his arms, and then I find myself outside the whole world. . . . He is in my heart, he is in heaven: both there and here he shows himself to me with equal glory."[24]

St. Symeon

Silence for Meditation

Psalm Fragment
For the word of the Lord is upright,
and all his work is done in faithfulness.
   Psalm 33:4

Questions to Ponder
- How has your understanding of the Word of God grown during these past three weeks of dwelling in the Word?
- How has your understanding of God the Word grown during these past three weeks of dwelling in the Word?
- Why do you think God chose to become human in the person of Jesus Christ? What difference does it make for you? For the world?
- What does it mean to be "saved"?

Prayer for Today
Save me, incarnate Word, from the power of sin and especially from my own sinfulness. Amen.

Day 20—Thursday

What has come into being in him was life, and the life was the light of all people.
   John 1:3b-4

John is still making connections to the creation story in Genesis 1. The first thing God created "in the beginning" was light, and then God went on to create life in all its wondrous variety. The Word through whom creation came to be, the Word who is Jesus, continues to bring life and light to our world today.

I have a cross necklace marked with two intersecting Greek words: *phos* (light) and *zoe* (life). The words, one vertical, one horizontal, overlap at the vowel in the center of the cross. Why are these two words intertwined? Is it just a clever coincidence of spelling that the artist noticed? Would any two words with a shared middle letter have worked? I think the words *phos* and *zoe* are intertwined because the realities they name, light and life, are intertwined, from the very beginning of creation. And the shared vowel is an omega, the last letter of the Greek alphabet, which suggests poetically that light and life will continue to be intertwined until the very end of the world.

For another example of how light and life are woven together, consider the process of photosynthesis, in which green plants use light as an energy source to produce organic compounds. As part of the process, plants remove carbon dioxide from the atmosphere and create oxygen as a by-product. For these reasons, scientists say that photosynthesis is essential for life on our planet. We could choose to think of this as "just science," or we can marvel at how the God who is our light and life wove these two things deeply into the very structures of the created world.

Biblical Wisdom
And the city has no need of sun or moon to shine on it, for the glory of God is its light, and its lamp is the Lamb. The nations will walk by its light, and the kings of the earth will bring their glory into it.
   Revelation 21:23-24

Theological Thoughts

"Thy strong word did cleave the darkness; At thy speaking it was done.
For created light we thank thee, While thine ordered seasons run.
. . . Praise to thee who light dost send!"[25]

ELW 511

Silence for Meditation

Psalm Fragment
Your word is a lamp to my feet
and a light to my path.
    Psalm 119:105

Questions to Ponder

- How many Scripture verses, hymns, or songs can you think of that have the word *light* in them?
- How many Scripture verses, hymns, or songs can you think of that have the word *life* in them?
- What do you think it means to say that the life is the light of *all* people?
- How can scientific knowledge help you to appreciate God's work and God's world?

Prayer for Today

God of growth and change, use me to transform your light into life for others. Amen.

Day 21—Friday

The light shines in the darkness, and the darkness did not overcome it.
    John 1:5

According to an old saying, it is better to light one candle than to curse the darkness. The problem, though, is that sometimes we don't even curse the darkness; we seek it out and embrace it. One of the ways the Scriptures describe human sinfulness is loving the darkness rather than the light. Just as literal darkness makes it difficult for us to see clearly, so too the darkness of sin makes it difficult for us to see the truth about ourselves and about others.

The sixteenth-century Spanish mystic St. John of the Cross wrote about a point on the spiritual journey that he called the dark night of the soul. He described a painful experience of spiritual darkness in which one feels abandoned by God. I once knew someone who described her own experience of the dark night of the soul as like being a planet in orbit around the sun. Sometimes, when she was closest to the sun, her faith life was warm and bright. But when she was at the most distant point of the orbit, she felt far from God, enveloped in cold and darkness. And there was nothing she could do to change her experience.

Whether we choose to live in darkness or whether we find ourselves in dark places against our will, there's good news for us in John's Gospel: "The light shines in the darkness, and the darkness did not overcome it." The creation story began with God's "Let there be light," but it didn't stop there. God separated the light from the darkness. God created the moon and the stars to provide light even during the night. The good news is not just that God created the light, but that God guarantees that light will triumph over darkness. When Jesus descends into hell after the crucifixion, he demonstrates beyond all doubt that there is no place where God's light cannot shine.

But the good news doesn't end there either. Jesus tells his disciples, "You are the light of world." We present a candle when someone is baptized, repeating Jesus' challenge to "Let your light so shine before others that they may see your good works and glorify your Father in heaven." Through us, God continues to shine light in the darkness, and the darkness cannot overcome it.

Biblical Wisdom
Again Jesus spoke to them, saying, "I am the light of the world. Whoever follows me will never walk in darkness but will have the light of life."
John 8:12

Theological Thoughts

"Your Word meant life triumphant hurled
In splendor through your broken world;
Since light awoke and life began,
You made for us a holy plan."[26]

Martin Franzmann, LBW 396

Silence for Meditation

Psalm Fragment
The unfolding of your words gives light;
it imparts understanding to the simple.
Psalm 119:130

Questions to Ponder

- How have you experienced God in your darkest times?
- What things have been most helpful to you in these times? Are there Scripture passages that have been especially meaningful for you?
- Where is there darkness in the world today?

Prayer for Today

Radiant God, help me to shine your light into all the dark places of this world.
Amen.

Day 22—Saturday

But to all who received him, who believed in his name, he gave power to become children of God, who were born, not of blood or of the will of the flesh or of the will of man, but of God.
John 1:12-13

My friends who are adoptive parents generally don't like to use the adjective *adopted*. If asked, "Is this your adopted child?" they tend to respond simply, "This is our child." Once a child is born, the reality of the child is more important than the length of the labor or the difficulty of the delivery. Similarly, once a child has been adopted, the child now is simply a member of the family. Exactly how he or she became a member of the family doesn't seem to matter. The person is more important than the process.

John does point to one aspect of the adoption process that's worth mentioning: the element of choice. John, of course, is talking about God's choice, not ours. God chooses to welcome us as members of the family. This isn't something that happens naturally. It's a choice. It's a whole series of choices. God in Christ chose to enter into our humanity personally. Jesus chose to carry a cross, to suffer and die for our sake. God chose to raise Jesus up from death. God chose—and chooses—to be gracious.

The word translated "power" in John 1:12 is somewhat misleading. We tend to equate power with force, but a better translation might be "authority." The word *authority* conveys a sense of legitimacy. Someone with the authority doesn't just have the ability to do something, but has the right to do so. The concept of authority also implies an element of freedom: someone with authority chooses how to act.

Obviously, God has authority, in our lives and over the whole creation. In the history of Israel and in the life, death, and resurrection of Jesus, God has chosen to use that authority for our benefit. What's even more remarkable is that God also chooses to share that authority with believers. Through faith in Christ Jesus, we have been made full members of the family. Each time we gather with other Christians, we are part of the family reunion of grace.

Biblical Wisdom

And because you are children, God has sent the Spirit of his Son into our hearts, crying, "Abba! Father!" So you are no longer a slave but a child, and if a child then also an heir, through God.

Galatians 4:6-7

Theological Thoughts

"My creatures should see and know that I wish nothing but their good, through the blood of my only begotten Son, in which they are washed from their iniquities. By this blood, they are enabled to know my truth: how, in order to give them eternal life, I created them in my image and likeness and re-created them by grace with the blood of my Son, making them my children by adoption."[27]

Catherine of Siena

Silence for Meditation

Psalm Fragment
Remember your word to your servant,
in which you have made me hope.
    Psalm 119:49

Questions to Ponder

- What does it mean for you to think of yourself as a son or daughter of God?
- What is the relationship between faith and authority? What does it mean to you to have authority as a Christian?
- What do you think John 1:12-13 has to say to people who do not believe in Jesus?

Prayer for Today
Father, thank you for adopting me into your family for the sake of your Son, my Brother, Jesus Christ. Amen.

Day 23—Monday

And the Word became flesh and lived among us . . . full of grace and truth.
    John 1:14

Words are a means of communication. They come in many forms and they carry many different messages. We use words to convey information. We can use words to affirm and we can also use words to wound.

In the musical *My Fair Lady*, Eliza Doolittle sings to her suitor, Freddy Eynsford-Hill, about being "sick of words." "If you're in love, show me!" she demands.

"Showing us" is exactly what God does in the incarnation. Words of love become Word of Love, in the flesh.

Throughout the Old Testament, God called prophets to speak the word to the people. But time and again, God's people proved hard of hearing. They refused to listen to God's message. The prophets themselves were often reluctant messengers, not wanting the responsibility of speaking God's word. The prophetic word was not enough; an incarnate Word was needed. "Show me!"

When Lutherans talk about the Word of God we mean a very specific kind of communication. The Word, we say, is a "means of grace." What God most wants us to hear and to experience is the gracious good news of Jesus Christ, crucified and risen for our sake. God's Word becomes incarnate to love and to save us. The Word becomes flesh and dwells among us, not to convey information about God but to give life!

Just as God sent prophets before the coming of Jesus, so too the risen Christ commissioned apostles as messengers after his resurrection. The witness of these prophets and apostles is recorded for us in the Old and New Testaments. But the witness is not finished yet. We who have heard the good news of the Word made flesh are called to share that good news with others. God's Word continues to dwell among us throughout our Christian life. And our words, when we share Christ's love with others, are also "full of grace and truth." Show, and tell!

Biblical Wisdom
For in him all the fullness of God was pleased to dwell, and through him God was pleased to reconcile to himself all things, whether on earth or in heaven, by making peace through the blood of his cross.
Colossians 1:19-20

Theological Thoughts
"Thy strong Word bespeaks us righteous; Bright with thine own holiness, Glorious now, we press toward glory, And our lives our hopes confess."[28]
ELW 511

Silence for Meditation

Psalm Fragment
He sent out his word and healed them,
and delivered them from destruction.
    Psalm 107:20

Questions to Ponder

- How do your words become flesh? How do you use words to wound and to heal?
- Are people ever sick of your words, or do they want to hear more from you? What should you do about this?
- How comfortable are you thinking about yourself as an apostle?

Prayer for Today

Incarnate God, guide my words that I may speak your Word faithfully to others. Amen.

Day 24—Tuesday

. . . and we have seen his glory, the glory as of a father's only son, full of grace and truth.
    John 1:14

In the ancient world, the title "son of God" was not unique. It could be used to refer to kings who were thought to have the favor of the gods. Because of this, it was important for early Christians to be sure that their creeds were clear about who Jesus is and what we mean when we say he is the Son of God. In the Apostles' Creed, we say that Jesus is "God's only Son, our Lord." The Nicene Creed expands this description, identifying Jesus as "the only Son of God, eternally begotten of the Father, God from God, Light from Light, true God from true God." The point is clear. As Son of God, Jesus is unique. Applied to Jesus, Son of God is not an honorary title, for he shares in God's divine nature itself.

But in the Scriptures as well as the creeds, the focus on who Jesus is quickly turns into a focus on what Jesus did. Martin Luther was critical of Christians who spent more time contemplating God's power and majesty than reflecting on what Jesus accomplished through his life, death, and resurrection. Luther called the former emphasis a "theology of glory." He was convinced that we could not know God directly, in glory, but only as God chose to be known, in Jesus. Although a hymn with this title was written several hundred years later, perhaps we could best describe Luther's emphasis with the words "In the Cross of Christ I Glory."

Jesus Christ is the only-begotten Son of God, but as we read several days ago, Jesus freely chooses to share his position in the family with us. We see God's glory in the crucified and risen one, and we are called to reflect God's glory in the broken places of the world.

Biblical Wisdom
Let the same mind be in you that was in Christ Jesus, who, though he was in the form of God, did not regard equality with God as something to be exploited, but emptied himself, taking the form of a slave, being born in human likeness.
Philippians 2:5-7

Theological Thoughts
"Who ever saw, who ever heard of the infinite God dwelling in a womb? Heaven is not large enough for him, yet a womb was not too small for him. He was born of woman—this God who is not only God, this man who is not merely man. . . . Had the Word not dwelt in a womb, the flesh would never have sat on the throne."[29]
St. Proclus

Silence for Meditation

Psalm Fragment
Remember me, O Lord, when you show favor to your people; help me when you deliver them; that I may see the prosperity of your chosen ones,

that I may rejoice in the gladness of your nation, that I may glory in your heritage.
    Psalm 106:4-5

Questions to Ponder

- How does the Christian understanding of glory differ from society's understanding of glory?
- What passages in the Apostles' or Nicene Creed have the most personal meaning for you?

More Questions to Ponder

This is the end of the fourth week of your Lenten journey with the Word. As you reflect back on the week, what themes do you notice? When in the past week have you most clearly felt God's presence?

Prayer for Today

"God of grace and glory of glory, on your people pour your pow'r. . . . Let the gift of your salvation be our glory evermore."[30] Amen.
Harry Emerson Fosdick, ELW 705

Journey Week Five:
The Word Sustains

Days 25–28

Comfort, O comfort my people, says your God. Speak tenderly to Jerusalem, and cry to her that she has served her term, that her penalty is paid, that she has received from the Lord's hand double for all her sins.

A voice cries out: "In the wilderness prepare the way of the Lord, make straight in the desert a highway for our God. Every valley shall be lifted up, and every mountain and hill be made low; the uneven ground shall become level, and the rough places a plain. Then the glory of the Lord shall be revealed, and all people shall see it together, for the mouth of the Lord has spoken."

. . . The grass withers, the flower fades; but the word of our God will stand forever.

    Isaiah 40:1-5, 8

Days 29–30

Ho, everyone who thirsts, come to the waters; and you that have no money, come, buy and eat! Come, buy wine and milk without money and without price. Why do you spend your money for that which is not bread, and your labor for that which does not satisfy? Listen carefully to me, and eat what is good, and delight yourselves in rich food. Incline your ear, and come to me; listen, so that you may live. I will make with you an everlasting covenant, my steadfast, sure love for David.

. . . For as the rain and the snow come down from heaven, and do not return there until they have watered the earth, making it bring forth and sprout, giving seed to the sower and bread to the eater, so shall my word be that goes out from my mouth; it shall not return to me empty, but it shall accomplish that which I purpose, and succeed in the thing for which I sent it.

Isaiah 55:1-3, 10-11

Day 25—Wednesday

Comfort, O comfort my people, says your God. Speak tenderly to Jerusa-
lem, and cry to her that she has served her term, that her penalty is paid,
that she has received from the LORD's hand double for all her sins.
  Isaiah 40:1-2

Some young children carry a comfort item with them wherever they go, like a blanket or a favorite stuffed animal. My youngest son's comfort item was a videotape of *The Lion King*. He slept with it, he carried it to Sunday school, and sometimes he even watched it. If you ask him today, "Why *The Lion King?*" he'll admit he doesn't know; it just had good associations for him.

As adults, there are times we crave comfort food. For some of us, it's the food of childhood, like macaroni and cheese or Mom's meatloaf and mashed potatoes. For others, it's something smooth, like cheesecake or ice cream. There's comfort in the food itself, to be sure, but the real comfort is in the memories. The food reminds us of people we love, familiar places, and good times.

When the prophet Isaiah is sent to proclaim God's message of comfort, what is he really offering? What keeps his message from being empty words? As James 2:15-16 points out, it's easy for us to say to a person in need, "Take care, stay warm," but unless we actually provide food, clothing, and shelter—real comfort—what good does it do?

Isaiah brings a message for the people of Israel living in exile in Babylon. It was bad enough to be conquered by an enemy people and carried off to another land. What was even worse was experiencing this exile as God's punishment for their faithlessness. Isaiah is able to bring real comfort into this hopeless situation because he brings a new word from God, the promise of a better future. The God who created the world, the God who liberated Israel from captivity in Egypt, has not abandoned Israel. God is still with them, and God can—and will—deliver them again from captivity.

Biblical Wisdom
When Israel was a child, I loved him, and out of Egypt I called my son. . . .
It was I who taught Ephraim to walk, I took them up in my arms; but they

did not know that I healed them. I led them with cords of human kindness,
with bands of love. I was to them like those who lift infants to their cheeks.
I bent down to them and fed them.
Hosea 11:1, 3-4

Theological Thoughts

"The mother can give her child to suck of her milk, but our precious Mother Jesus can feed us with himself, and does, most courteously and most tenderly, with the blessed sacrament, which is the precious food of true life. . . . The mother can lay her child tenderly to her breast, but our tender Mother Jesus can lead us easily into his blessed breast through his sweet open side, and show us there a part of the godhead and of the joys of heaven."[31]

Julian of Norwich

Silence for Meditation

Psalm Fragment
My soul melts away for sorrow;
strengthen me according to your word.
Psalm 119:28

Questions to Ponder

- What are your comfort objects or foods?
- In today's *Theological Thoughts*, Julian of Norwich describes Jesus as our mother. How do you respond to this? How does this kind of imagery help you to see God as our comforter?
- Have you ever felt hopeless or abandoned by God? What sustained you during those times?

Prayer for Today

Refresh me, Lord, with the true comfort food, your own body and blood, given in love for me. Amen.

Day 26—Thursday

> *A voice cries out: "In the wilderness prepare the way of the L*ORD*, make straight in the desert a highway for our God. Every valley shall be lifted up, and every mountain and hill be made low; the uneven ground shall become level, and the rough places a plain."*
> Isaiah 40:3-4

The initial verses of Isaiah 40 offer a word of comfort to Israel in exile, the promise of a new and better future. These next verses issue a call to prepare for that new future.

In the Small Catechism, Luther explains the Lord's Prayer petition "your kingdom come" this way: "In fact, God's kingdom comes on its own without our prayer, but we ask in this prayer that it may also come to us."[32] I think Luther offers us some insight into Isaiah's message. God's promised future for the people of Israel is sure, for no other reason than that God has promised it. God doesn't need their help—or ours. But the call to prepare is an enthusiastic expression of trust and anticipation. Despite the challenges and hardships of our present circumstances, we trust God's Word and we act our way into the future that God has promised!

The season of Lent is a time of preparation. In the church year, Lent precedes Easter, but historically Christians celebrated Easter first. Over time, the anticipation of Easter resulted in the development of the customs we associate with Lent. Lent was first used as a time of instruction for those who would be baptized at Easter. Lent was also used as a time of repentance for sinners whose offenses were particularly serious. Eventually Lent became a time for all Christians to prepare themselves for Good Friday and Easter.

Isaiah's call to put things right in anticipation of God's promised future is both all-embracing and ongoing. Just as we know that the vehicles we drive need occasional realignment, so too there are times when we need to readjust the alignment of our own lives. Let Lent be for you a time of reflection and, as needed, mid-course correction, all the while trusting that resurrection is coming!

Biblical Wisdom

"So when you are offering your gift at the altar, if you remember that your brother or sister has something against you, leave your gift there before the altar and go; first be reconciled to your brother or sister, and then come and offer your gift."

Matthew 5:23-24

Theological Thoughts

"Since that day God has been at work toward the mending of the creation. . . . The kingdom of God, the kingdom of heaven, stands for a mended creation with people and things—a social, economic, ecological reality. Thus, Jesus' miracles were not primarily signs of his power but acts of mending the creation, pushing back the frontier of Satan, healing minds and bodies, feeding, even counteracting the devastation of the premature death of the young and the needy."[33]

Krister Stendahl

Silence for Meditation

Psalm Fragment

He sends out his command to the earth;
his word runs swiftly.

Psalm 147:15

Questions to Ponder

- What in your life needs to be straightened out or mended? How can God's Word make a difference?
- What in your community needs to be straightened out or mended? How can God's Word make a difference?
- How does trusting that the future is in God's hands affect the choices you make in the present?

Prayer for Today

Righteous God, help me to align myself—and the world—to your will. Amen.

Day 27—Friday

> *"Then the glory of the* Lord *shall be revealed, and all people shall see it together, for the mouth of the* Lord *has spoken."*
> Isaiah 40:5

I can never read this verse without hearing the strains of Handel's "Messiah" accompanying it. We tend to think of this piece only as a Christmas production. But Handel's oratorio tells the whole story of salvation in three acts, taking us from Advent prophecies, through Lenten passion, to Easter triumph.

Isaiah's original message was that the glory of the Lord would be revealed through God's deliverance of the people of Israel from their exile in Babylon. In the New Testament, Matthew, Mark, and Luke build on this prophetic word by applying the verses we read yesterday to John the Baptist. This added layer of meaning is the reason Handel uses Isaiah 40 in Advent, as does the lectionary we use on Sundays. Read in Advent rather than in exile, today's verse points to the coming Messiah as the one in whom the glory of the Lord is finally and fully revealed.

When we read or hear these words in Lent, we are drawn more deeply into the mystery of the revealing of God's glory. What does this glory look like? The glory of the Lord, revealed in a tiny baby in a cattle stall? Not likely. The glory of the Lord, revealed in a condemned man hanging on a cross? Even less likely! What a strange kind of glory this is, revealed in the most unexpected places. And what a strange kind of faith we Christians have, who trust that this is really where God meets us.

Of course, Isaiah's words aren't only meant for believers. "All people shall see it together," he says boldly. In the Old Testament, God's mighty acts of deliverance always reveal a glory which is meant to be seen by Israel and by the other nations and peoples of the world. The life, death, and resurrection of Jesus Christ are also meant for the world to see, and so the risen Lord calls those who believe in him to be his witnesses. How are we doing? More than 2,500 years since the prophet's time, almost 2,000 years since the first Good Friday, how much longer will it be before all people recognize—and glory in—God the Deliverer?

Biblical Wisdom
"And I, when I am lifted up from the earth, will draw all people to myself."
  John 12:32

Theological Thoughts
"From the cross thy wisdom shining breaketh forth in conqu'ring might; from the cross forever beameth all thy bright redeeming light."[34]
  ELW 511

Silence for Meditation

Psalm Fragment
All the kings of the earth shall praise you, O Lord,
for they have heard the words of your mouth.
  Psalm 138:4

Questions to Ponder
- How can you help others to see and experience God's glory?
- What's different about how you see God's glory revealed at Christmas and at Easter?
- What's different about how you prepare for Christmas and how you prepare for Easter?

Prayer for Today
Creator God, thank you for showing me your glory through the creativity of artists and musicians as well as through your Word. Amen.

Day 28—Saturday

The grass withers, the flower fades; but the word of our God will stand forever.
  Isaiah 40:8

In the Harry Potter book series, the villain Lord Voldemort is often referred to as "he who must not be named." Many of the characters feel that even to speak the name of this evil wizard will somehow increase his power. Harry Potter, who has fought with Lord Voldemort more than once, is not afraid to say the name and encourages his friends to do so too, rather than letting their fears overwhelm them.

I'm on a personal crusade to eliminate the use of the phrase "passed away," especially in church. Christians, of all people, shouldn't need to refer to death with euphemisms. After all, we proclaim the promise of resurrection from the dead. We needn't soften the blow of death, because we worship a crucified and risen Lord who has conquered death itself.

When I wander through cemeteries, it's not the polished marble gravestones that I'm drawn to. It's the old weathered stones. Time has worn away the edges and some of the lettering. Moss grows in some of the grooves and cracks. There's an honesty to those old gravestones. The bodies buried there have experienced death and decay, and it seems only right that the markers of their lives should reflect the same vulnerability. Death isn't smooth and pretty. Why cover it up?

Death is a harsh reality, but as Christians we also believe that death is not the final word. The final word has already been spoken for each of us, when we were named and claimed by God in the sacrament of Holy Baptism. We confess that in baptism we were joined to Christ's death and resurrection. Martin Luther encouraged Christians to think of baptism as a daily dying to sin and the old self and as a daily rising to new life through God's grace. It's this baptismal confidence in the resurrection—Christ's and ours—that allows us to face sin and death full in the face.

> *Biblical Wisdom*
> *Do you not know that all of us who have been baptized into Christ Jesus were baptized into his death? Therefore we have been buried with him by baptism into death, so that, just as Christ was raised from the dead by the glory of the Father, so we too might walk in newness of life. For if we have been united with him in a death like his, we will certainly be united with him in a resurrection like his.*
> Romans 6:3-5

Theological Thoughts

"Just as the wooden branch of the vine, placed in the earth, bears fruit in its own time—and as the grain of wheat, falling into the ground and there dissolved, rises with great increase by the Spirit of God, who sustains all things . . . —so also our bodies which are nourished by it, and fall into the earth and are dissolved therein, shall rise at the proper time, the Word of God bestowing on them this rising again, to the glory of God the Father."[35]

St. Irenaeus of Lyons

Silence for Meditation

Psalm Fragment
My soul clings to the dust;
revive me according to your word.
Psalm 119:25

Questions to Ponder
- How comfortable are you talking about death?
- Does it make a difference whether you are talking about your own death or about someone else's death?

Prayer for Today
God, my maker and redeemer, help me to trust that in life and in death I belong to you. Amen.

Day 29—Monday

Incline your ear, and come to me; listen, so that you may live.
Isaiah 55:3a

I preached for several weeks in a congregation that used hymns to replace some of the parts of the liturgy. We sang "Lord, Let My Heart Be Good Soil" (ELW 512) before the first lesson and then sang stanzas 1 and 3 of "Drawn to the Light" (ELW 593) in place of an alleluia verse. Both hymns use first-person pronouns, which made the experience feel very personal. It was as if through our singing we were acknowledging that the Scripture lessons were addressed to each one of us.

Scientists tell us that the brain responds differently to music than to spoken language. One aspect of this is that it's easier to remember things we learn when they are accompanied by music. There are catchy tunes to help children memorize the books of the Bible as well as individual scriptural passages. Older adults, even when their memories have faded almost completely, often respond to a familiar hymn. So it makes sense to surround the hearing of the Word in our worship services with song, to open our minds and to reinforce the words that we hear.

The theme of this Lenten devotional book, Seven Wonders of the Word, calls to mind for me a phrase in John C. Ylvisaker's well-known hymn "Borning Cry" (ELW 732):

> "When you heard the wonder of the Word I was there to cheer you on;
> You were raised to praise the living Lord, to whom you now belong."

It's a hymn that's sung at baptisms, confirmations, weddings, and funerals. The stanzas take us on a journey through all of the stages of life, reminding us how God is present and active with us in every one of them. God's Word offers wisdom, love, everything we need, and it never stops amazing us. There's so much to listen to, so much to sing about!

Biblical Wisdom
Simon Peter answered him, "Lord, to whom can we go? You have the words of eternal life. We have come to believe and know that you are the Holy One of God."
John 6:68-69

Theological Thoughts
"Silence is the simple stillness of the individual under the Word of God. We are silent before hearing the Word because our thoughts are already directed to the Word, as a child is quiet when he enters his father's room. We are silent after hearing the Word because the Word is still speaking and dwelling within us. We are silent at the beginning of the day because God should have the first word, and

we are silent before going to sleep because the last word also belongs to God. We keep silence solely for the sake of the Word . . . to honor and receive it."[36]

Dietrich Bonhoeffer

Silence for Meditation

Psalm Fragment
Let my cry come before you, O Lᴏʀᴅ;
give me understanding according to your word.
　　Psalm 119:169

Questions to Ponder
- How do you prepare yourself to receive God's Word?
- How is music a part of your devotional life?
- What Bible passages or hymns have you memorized, or would you like to memorize? What do they mean to you?

Prayer for Today
Lord, let my life and my heart be good soil, open to the seed of your Word. Amen.

Day 30—Tuesday

For as the rain and the snow come down from heaven, and do not return there until they have watered the earth, making it bring forth and sprout, giving seed to the sower and bread to the eater, so shall my word be that goes out from my mouth; it shall not return to me empty, but it shall accomplish that which I purpose, and succeed in the thing for which I sent it.
　　Isaiah 55:10-11

These verses are another reminder of the creation story in Genesis 1—God creates through the Word—but Isaiah shows us a slightly different perspective. Throughout the first chapter of Genesis, God says "Let there be," and things happen. God's Word has direct results. Isaiah knows that God's Word will accomplish God's purposes, but in these verses he also shows how God works indirectly. The rain and the snow, the earth and the seasons, are all things God created in the beginning. They are also now things God uses to continue God's creative work in the world. The God through whose Word the world was first created continues to sustain the world, through the Word itself and through the natural processes that have been set in motion.

Our experience of God's creative and sustaining Word is typically more like Isaiah's than like the creation story. We hear the Word and trust the promise, but the results are rarely immediate. God uses the skills of physicians, nurses, and surgeons to heal more frequently than God works miracles. Most of us discern God's call for our lives through our experiences, our education, and in conversation with others rather than through direct prophetic address. But it is God's Word and work nonetheless, embedded in the created order and embodied in others.

Biblical Wisdom

What then is Apollos? What is Paul? Servants through whom you came to believe, as the Lord assigned to each. I planted, Apollos watered, but God gave the growth.
  1 Corinthians 3:5-6

Theological Thoughts

"For faith must come freely without compulsion. Take myself as an example. I opposed indulgences and all the papists, but never with force. I simply taught, preached, and wrote God's Word; otherwise I did nothing. And while I slept [cf. Mark 4:26-29], or drank Wittenberg beer with my friends Philip and Amsdorf, the Word so greatly weakened the papacy that no prince or emperor ever inflicted such losses upon it. I did nothing; the Word did everything."[37]
  Martin Luther

Silence for Meditation

Psalm Fragment
This is the Lord's doing;
it is marvelous in our eyes.
This is the day that the Lord has made;
let us rejoice and be glad in it.
> Psalm 118:23-24

Questions to Ponder

- Where have you experienced the fulfillment of God's Word in your life? Where are you still waiting for fulfillment?
- How does God use us to accomplish God's purposes in the world?
- What do you think success looks like for God?

More Questions to Ponder

This is the end of the fifth week of your Lenten journey with the Word. As you reflect back on the week, what themes do you notice? When in the past week have you most clearly felt God's presence?

Prayer for Today

Bountiful God, use me to plant and to water in your garden, the earth, and give me the patience to wait for you to give growth. Amen.

Journey Week Six: The Word Shapes

Days 31–33

> Then Jesus said to the Jews who had believed in him, "If you continue in my word, you are truly my disciples; and you will know the truth, and the truth will make you free." They answered him, "We are descendants of Abraham and have never been slaves to anyone. What do you mean by saying, 'You will be made free'?"
>
> Jesus answered them, "Very truly, I tell you, everyone who commits sin is a slave to sin. The slave does not have a permanent place in the household; the son has a place there forever. So if the Son makes you free, you will be free indeed.
>> John 8:31-36

Days 34-36

> But as for you, continue in what you have learned and firmly believed, knowing from whom you learned it, and how from childhood you have known the sacred writings that are able to instruct you for salvation

through faith in Christ Jesus. All scripture is inspired by God and is useful for teaching, for reproof, for correction, and for training in righteousness, so that everyone who belongs to God may be proficient, equipped for every good work.

2 Timothy 3:14-17

Day 31—Wednesday

Then Jesus said to the Jews who had believed in him, "If you continue in my word, you are truly my disciples."
   John 8:31

What does it mean to be a disciple?

A search for "discipleship" on amazon.com yields well over twenty thousand results. Many of the books for sale offer a step-by-step guide, a kind of spiritual self-help approach. But Christian discipleship is hardly a do-it-yourself project. In the ancient world, would-be disciples spent time listening to several rabbis or teachers before deciding which one to affiliate with. But things are different with Jesus. The disciples do not seek out this teacher. This teacher, Jesus, chooses his disciples himself and calls them to come with him. Jesus initiates; we respond.

It's easy to focus on discipleship in terms of what we do. After all, *discipleship* and *discipline* share the same root. The New Testament understanding of discipleship, however, focuses not on our behavior but on the relationship between the disciple and the teacher, a close interpersonal relationship that forms and shapes the identity of the disciples.

It's important for us to hear that Jesus' words are spoken to people who have already believed. We know this not only because the text tells us so but also because the encouragement to *continue* in Jesus' Word only makes sense when it is addressed to those who are *already* shaped by that Word. Jesus initiates the relationship; we respond. How we choose to live out our Christian faith matters. But before we can follow Jesus, we need to be with Jesus, faithfully sitting and listening at his feet, like Mary (Luke 10:38-42). We are able to continue in his Word only when we are first fed with that Word by God's gracious initiative.

Biblical Wisdom
"Go therefore and make disciples of all nations, baptizing them in the name of the Father and of the Son and of the Holy Spirit, and teaching them to obey everything that I have commanded you. And remember, I am with you always, to the end of the age."
   Matthew 28:19-20

Theological Thoughts

"Be sure, moreover, that you do not make Christ into a Moses, as if Christ did nothing more than teach and provide examples as the other saints do, as if the gospel were simply a textbook of teachings or laws. . . . The chief article and foundation of the gospel is that before you take Christ as an example, you accept and recognize him as a gift, as a present that God has given you and that is your own."[38]

Martin Luther

Silence for Meditation

Psalm Fragment
Lord, you have been our dwelling place in all generations.
Before the mountains were brought forth,
or ever you had formed the earth and the world,
from everlasting to everlasting you are God.
    Psalm 90:1-2

Questions to Ponder

- What does discipleship mean to you?
- How do you understand the relationship between discipleship and discipline?
- According to the Gospels, Jesus' first disciples often misunderstood him. Is this discouraging or comforting for you as you think about your own discipleship?
- What does it mean to "continue" in Jesus' Word?

Prayer for Today

Teacher, call me to yourself, form me in your Word, and send me forth as your disciple. Amen.

Day 32—Thursday

Then Jesus said to the Jews who had believed in him, "If you continue in my word, you are truly my disciples; and you will know the truth, and the truth will make you free."
John 8:31-32

I chose "The truth shall make you free" as my confirmation verse. I had recently read a novel in which the heroine's name was Verity, which means truth. As a naïve teenager, I had a somewhat romanticized notion of truth as an ideal virtue. My pastor wisely insisted that I use the full two verses as my confirmation text, not just the sound bite I liked. What I grew to understand is that Jesus is not talking about truth in the abstract, as a quality that has value in and of itself. Later in John's Gospel, Jesus identifies himself as the Truth! When Jesus says to those who believe in him, "you will know the truth, and the truth will make you free," he's not defending the claim that honesty is the best policy. He's pointing them to himself, as the source of truth and the source of freedom.

The verb *continue* has rich connotations in Greek. It can also be translated as "remain" or "dwell." It's the same word Jesus uses when he describes the relationship between himself and the disciples with the image of the vine and the branches. Discipleship understood this way is an organic relationship. We who by faith are rooted in Christ Jesus have been watered in baptism. We receive rich nutrients through the sacrament of communion. When we are healthy—connected to the root, nourished, and watered—then Jesus' Word, like the sap in a plant, becomes the very lifeblood running through our veins.

In a society that prizes independence, being rooted may sound like the very opposite of freedom. But just as Jesus calls us to a deeper understanding of truth, he offers us a deeper understanding of freedom as well. Songwriter Kris Kristofferson famously described freedom as "just another word for nothin' left to lose." But what could be more truly freeing than the life Christ shares with us, together with the promise that nothing can uproot us!

Biblical Wisdom

"I am the way, and the truth, and the life. No one comes to the Father except through me."
　　John 14:6

Theological Thoughts

"It is only because we follow Jesus that we can be genuinely truthful, for then he reveals to us our sin upon the cross. The cross is God's truth about us, and therefore it is the only power which can make us truthful. When we know the cross we are no longer afraid of the truth."[39]
　　Dietrich Bonhoeffer

Silence for Meditation

Psalm Fragment

But their delight is in the law of the LORD, and on his law they meditate day and night.
They are like trees planted by streams of water, which yield their fruit in its season, and their leaves do not wither. In all that they do, they prosper.
　　Psalm 1:2-3

Questions to Ponder

- What kind of freedom is Jesus talking about?
- Does your Christian faith ever seem limiting to you? When is it most freeing?
- How can we talk meaningfully about truth in a culture heavily influenced by relativism, or the belief that everything depends upon the situation?

Prayer for Today

Incarnate Word, as you have come to dwell among us, help us now to dwell within you. Amen.

Day 33—Friday

They answered him, "We are descendants of Abraham and have never been slaves to anyone. What do you mean by saying, 'You will be made free'?" Jesus answered them, "Very truly, I tell you, everyone who commits sin is a slave to sin. The slave does not have a permanent place in the household; the son has a place there forever. So if the Son makes you free, you will be free indeed."
John 8:33-36

We often begin worship by confessing that "we are in bondage to sin and cannot free ourselves." There's an even deeper problem, I think. Sometimes we don't even recognize that we're in bondage, let alone have the ability to free ourselves from it. I think that's the situation for the Jewish believers Jesus is talking with in this passage, who say they "have never been slaves to anyone"! What about the years of slavery the Israelites spent in Egypt? What about the forced exile to Babylon? And what about the fact that first-century Judea itself was an occupied territory under the control of the Roman Empire? Who are they trying to fool: Jesus or themselves?

I'm not sure whether the people really wanted an answer from Jesus. Their response sounds almost like the quick dismissal we give to telemarketers, "No thanks. We're not interested in what you have to offer." But Jesus is unwilling just to let them walk away. He keeps the conversation going, and not just in these few short verses. Jesus and the people argue back and forth for the rest of this chapter in John. They challenge his faith, they challenge his sanity, and they challenge his youth before they decide they have finally heard enough, and then they threaten to stone him.

This may sound strange, but sometimes when I hang up on a telemarketer, I imagine that they'll call back and attempt to persuade me. Obviously, that doesn't happen; they simply move on to the next number. But I'm so grateful that Jesus doesn't let us hang up on him! Jesus has the gracious persistence that I am fearful of with telemarketers. He speaks. We respond with an excuse. He speaks again. We ask questions. He speaks again. We complain. He speaks again. In this passage and in our lives, Jesus has the last word.

Biblical Wisdom
*Jesus answered her, "If you knew the gift of God, and who it is that is
saying to you, 'Give me a drink,' you would have asked him, and he would
have given you living water."*
John 4:10

Theological Thoughts
"Lo, on those who dwelt in darkness, Dark as night and deep as death,
Broke the light of Thy salvation, Breathed thine own life-breathing breath."[40]
ELW 511

Silence for Meditation

Psalm Fragment
*Then I shall have an answer for those who taunt me,
for I trust in your word.*
Psalm 119:42

Questions to Ponder
- Are there things in your life that threaten to enslave you? How can the living Word make a difference?
- How does your own experience of home and family shape your understanding of what it means to be part of the household of faith?
- How comfortable are you asking others—and God—for what you need?

Prayer for Today
Patient and loving God, thank you for allowing us to wrestle with you, and thank you for never giving up on us. Amen.

Day 34—Saturday

But as for you, continue in what you have learned and firmly believed,
knowing from whom you learned it, and how from childhood you have
known the sacred writings that are able to instruct you for salvation
through faith in Christ Jesus.
    2 Timothy 3:14-15

In some Christian traditions, it's important to have a conversion experience—a particular event, at a particular time and place, which one can point to as the life-changing moment at which one experienced the grace of God or made a decision to turn one's life over to Christ. Sometimes I hear from recent college graduates, former students of mine, who are being pressured by friends to be baptized again as an expression of their own mature faith commitment. I typically remind them that baptism is about God's promises to us, not about our promises to God. We can continue to reaffirm and build on that baptismal foundation throughout our lives, but baptism itself can't really be repeated.

I've always been grateful to my parents for raising me in the faith. I can't remember a time when I didn't know that I was a baptized and beloved child of God. In my experience, growing in the Christian faith has not been a dramatic story full of twists and turns but a gradual unfolding of what I've known all along—sort of as the petals on a flower continue to unfold in the sunlight.

My parents chose three godparents for me, none of whom was able to be physically present on my baptismal day, but each of whom was spiritually present for me throughout my growing up years. As I grew, it was a blessing for me to have these three Christian adults in my life who were trustworthy and who loved me not because we were related but because they had each made a faith commitment to be there for me.

In the baptismal liturgy, we ask parents and sponsors to accept the responsibility to place the Holy Scriptures into the hands of these new Christians, to bring them to worship, and to teach them to pray. As we grow, we are able to assume these responsibilities for ourselves, as adult Christians. But I remain grateful for 2 Timothy's reminder to honor both the written Word of God and the people who have been living instruments of the Word in our lives.

Biblical Wisdom
Keep these words that I am commanding you today in your heart. Recite
them to your children and talk about them when you are at home and
when you are away, when you lie down and when you rise.
Deuteronomy 6:6-7

Theological Thoughts
"When it comes to praying scripture, to reading it as the book of God and God's people, Christians do need to pray the whole of scripture as though it is to be understood through a single interpretive lens. That lens is the person of Jesus."[41]
Roberta C. Bondi

Silence for Meditation

Psalm Fragment
You are my hiding place and my shield;
I hope in your word.
Psalm 119:114

Questions to Ponder
· What do you remember about the religious instruction and faith formation you received as a child?
· How has your faith changed over time?
· What role have godparents or faith mentors played in your life? If you have godchildren, what role do you play in their lives?

Prayer for Today
Lord, keep me steadfast in your Word, and use me as a faithful teacher in the lives of others. Amen.

Day 35—Monday

All scripture is inspired by God and is useful for teaching, for reproof, for correction, and for training in righteousness.
2 Timothy 3:16

Our college library has a coffee shop in it. When the library was renovated and expanded in the 1990s, the director insisted we remember that the purpose of a library is to facilitate learning, not to protect the collection. The library should be a comfortable place to settle in and work for a while, not a museum for books. Learning requires learners, and if the ability to take a coffee break without leaving the library will help keep students at their studies, it's worth providing.

Even more so than library books, the Scriptures are meant to be used! The Greek text of 2 Timothy 3:16 makes it clear that the adjectives *inspired* and *useful* belong together as a single phrase; they are not two separate points that happen to be joined into one sentence. When we confess that the Scriptures are both "inspired and useful," we see the Bible not just in relationship to other books but in relationship to us, its readers and hearers!

The word *inspiration* literally means having spirit or breath within. When we say that great literature or art is inspired, we are describing the creativity of the human spirit. When we talk about divine inspiration, it is the Holy Spirit to whom we refer. It's helpful, I think, to reflect on scriptural inspiration in the same way we reflected on God's act of creation earlier in this Lenten journey. Creation, we said, doesn't refer only to what God did "in the beginning" but also to what God continues to do in the world God has made. Similarly, inspiration can refer not only to how the Scriptures came to be written but also to how God continues to breathe the life-giving Holy Spirit into the texts as we encounter them today—and to how the Holy Spirit continues to breathe in us, shaping us as God's faithful people.

Biblical Wisdom
Or do you not know that your body is a temple of the Holy Spirit within you, which you have from God, and that you are not your own?
1 Corinthians 6:19

Theological Thoughts

"The Bible as the written Word of God needs to be interpreted so that we can hear clearly what God is saying to us through it. God's Word comes to us through human words, written by human authors, during the course of human history. We can agree that the Scriptures are the inspired Word of God, but it is not always easy to agree on what a particular passage means for Christians today. The same Spirit who inspired the writing of the Scriptures is at work in the community of believers inspiring us as we study and apply God's Word."[42]

Kathryn A. Kleinhans

Silence for Meditation

Psalm Fragment
How sweet are your words to my taste,
sweeter than honey to my mouth!
    Psalm 119:103

Questions to Ponder

- What does inspiration mean to you? How is the inspiration of the Scriptures related to other kinds of inspiration?
- In what ways and what situations have you found the Scriptures most useful for you personally?
- How many Bibles do you have, and where are they located in your home? Does their location say anything about how they are used?

Prayer for Today

Holy Spirit, breathe through the Scriptures into me, shaping me for your purposes. Amen.

Day 36—Tuesday

. . . so that everyone who belongs to God may be proficient, equipped for every good work.
    2 Timothy 3:17

My husband's grandfather was a carpenter by trade. His grandfather's tools are among my husband's prize possessions. Through his grandfather's legacy, he is, you might say, "equipped for every good work," at least in the woodworking category.

I teach at Wartburg College, one of the colleges and universities of the Evangelical Lutheran Church in America. When I talk with students about the importance of a liberal arts education, I also use the language of tools. While students typically want to focus on their major subject and their intended career, it's the basic academic tools of reading, writing, critical thinking, clear and persuasive speech, and so forth that are their best preparation for the future. Jobs and interests will change over time, but a solid educational foundation provides the skills to change along with them.

We find a powerful description of the Christian's spiritual tools in Ephesians 6:10-17. "The whole armor of God" includes "the belt of truth," "the breastplate of righteousness," "the shield of faith," "the helmet of salvation," and "the sword of the Spirit, which is the word of God." We're also given this advice: "As shoes for your feet put on whatever will make you ready to proclaim the gospel of peace." I'm drawn in by the word *whatever*. The other spiritual tools named in this passage are more specific. Truth, righteousness, faith, salvation, and the word of God are essential items for Christian life and work. But this "whatever" is open-ended: whatever will equip you to share the good news goes into your toolbox. That may be different for you than for me. That may be different at different times or in different situations. The possibilities are limitless.

The Holy Spirit uses the Word to shape us, and through the Word the Holy Spirit equips us with the tools we need to serve others in Jesus' name. What a marvelous line of work we are in!

> *Biblical Wisdom*
> *Jesus said to them again, "Peace be with you. As the Father has sent me, so I send you." When he had said this, he breathed on them and said to them, "Receive the Holy Spirit."*
> John 20:21-22

Theological Thoughts

"A source of spiritual delight is the Word of God contained in Holy Scripture. In Scripture is found the ultimate truth that enlightens the mind, which, as mind, has truth as its object. Moreover, there is intense sweetness and grace in the words of Scripture, which draw like a great magnet the hearts of the readers to agree with them and to be persuaded."[43]

St. Nicodemos of the Holy Mountain

Silence for Meditation

Psalm Fragment
The LORD is my strength and my shield;
In him my heart trusts;
so I am helped, and my heart exults,
and with my song I give thanks to him.
    Psalm 28:7

Questions to Ponder
· What spiritual tools do you use most frequently?
· How proficient do you feel in your life as a Christian? How would you like to improve?

More Questions to Ponder

This is the end of the sixth week of your Lenten journey with the Word. As you reflect back on the week, what themes do you notice? When in the past week have you most clearly felt God's presence?

Prayer for Today

Lord of the harvest, you call me to work in your vineyard. Give me a willing heart and skilled hands as I labor in your service. Amen.

Journey Week Seven: The Word Sends

Days 37-40

But the righteousness that comes from faith says, "Do not say in your heart, 'Who will ascend into heaven?'" (that is, to bring Christ down) "or 'Who will descend into the abyss?'" (that is, to bring Christ up from the dead). But what does it say? "The word is near you, on your lips and in your heart" (that is, the word of faith that we proclaim); because if you confess with your lips that Jesus is Lord and believe in your heart that God raised him from the dead, you will be saved. For one believes with the heart and so is justified, and one confesses with the mouth and so is saved. The scripture says, "No one who believes in him will be put to shame." For there is no distinction between Jew and Greek; the same Lord is Lord of all and is generous to all who call on him. For, "Everyone who calls on the name of the Lord shall be saved."

But how are they to call on one in whom they have not believed? And how are they to believe in one of whom they have never heard? And how are they to hear without someone to proclaim him? And how are they to proclaim him unless they are sent? As it is written, "How beautiful are the feet

of those who bring good news!" But not all have obeyed the good news; for Isaiah says, "Lord, who has believed our message?" So faith comes from what is heard, and what is heard comes through the word of Christ.
    Romans 10:6-17

Day 37—Wednesday

"The word is near you, on your lips and in your heart" (that is, the word of
faith that we proclaim); because if you confess with your lips that Jesus is
Lord and believe in your heart that God raised him from the dead, you will
be saved.
Romans 10:8b-9

We are nearing the end of our Lenten journey. We have spent the past six weeks dwelling in God's Word and letting God's Word dwell in us. The Word has created and recreated us, called us, and commanded us. The Word who saves us has also sustained and shaped us. Now, as we enter into the heart of Holy Week, Paul's words to the Romans help us to focus our hearts and minds as the Word sends us, with Jesus, toward the cross.

Paul's epistle to the Romans was written to Christians he had never met. In many of his other letters, Paul is able to remind his audience of the message he himself had shared with them during their time together, but this time it's different. While Paul is eager to visit the Roman Christians, he knows that their faith does not depend on him. The Word that Paul and his coworkers preach is the Word that the Christians in Rome already know and trust. Paul may be far from Rome, but the Word is as close to them as it can be: they have it on their lips and in their hearts, whether or not their preacher is with them.

It's easy for congregations in a time of pastoral vacancy to feel that their ministry is on hold. When the new pastor comes, things will get going again. But ministry does not depend on the presence of a pastor; ministry depends on—and is empowered by—God's living Word. That Word is near to each of us. We heard it first in baptism. We hear it again in worship, both in spoken word and in song. We read it for ourselves when we study and pray the Scriptures. This Word that is deeply etched into our hearts cries out to be spoken to others. God has equipped us not only for ourselves but to reach out and serve others. God's living, life-giving Word has come to us in order to send us out into God's world to share the good news.

Biblical Wisdom
Let the word of Christ dwell in you richly; teach and admonish one another in all wisdom; and with gratitude in your hearts sing psalms, hymns, and spiritual songs to God.
    Colossians 3:16

Theological Thoughts
"The nature of water is soft, the nature of stone is hard; but if a bottle is hung above a stone letting water drip down, it wears away the stone. It is like that with the word of God; it is soft and our heart is hard; but if someone hears the word of God often, it will break open his heart to the fear of God."[44]
    The Desert Fathers: Sayings of the Early Christian Monks

Silence for Meditation

Psalm Fragment
Hear my prayer, O God;
give ear to the words of my mouth.
    Psalm 54:2

Questions to Ponder
- When do you feel that God's Word is most near to you?
- How challenging do you find it to move the Word from your heart to your lips?
- How does God's Word connect you to other Christians, near and far?

Prayer for Today
"Lord, speak to us, that we may speak. . . . Oh, lead us, Lord, that we may lead."[45]
Amen.
    Frances R. Havergal

Day 38—Maundy Thursday

But how are they to call on one in whom they have not believed? And how are they to believe in one of whom they have never heard? And how are they to hear without someone to proclaim him? And how are they to proclaim him unless they are sent?
Romans 10:14-15a

On Maundy Thursday, Jesus shared a meal with his disciples and gave them "a new commandment," to love one another as he loved them (John 13:34). This meal has many names. When we call it "the Last Supper," we are describing the final meal Jesus shared with his disciples before his betrayal, arrest, and execution. When we call it "the Lord's Supper," we are emphasizing that Jesus is the host and we are the guests. When we call it "eucharist," we are reminding ourselves that it is an act of thanksgiving for God's gracious gift, and when we call it "communion," we are naming the way in which this meal unites us with Jesus and with our fellow believers.

Martin Luther sometimes called the sacrament "a new testament" in Jesus' blood. He explained this name by referring to the familiar concept of a last will and testament. A testament, he said, is a promise made by someone who is about to die. It names who the heirs are and what their inheritance will be. It becomes effective only upon the death of the person who gave it. Jesus' words at the Last Supper, on the night before his death, fill in the details. The inheritance is the forgiveness of sins. The heirs are "for you" (in Luke and 1 Corinthians) and "for many" (in Matthew and Mark).

This inheritance is really ours now, but not ours alone. With his new commandment, Jesus made us the executors of his testament. As executors, we have the responsibility of carrying out his dying wish. We have the responsibility of locating the other heirs and making sure they receive their full share of the inheritance, too. The message of forgiveness, new life, and salvation is ours to proclaim.

The communion liturgy ends with the words "Go in peace, serve the Lord" or "Go in peace, share the good news." We serve our Lord when we share the good news of his love with others. The inheritance is more than enough to go around!

Biblical Wisdom

For I am not ashamed of the gospel; it is the power of God for salvation to everyone who has faith, to the Jew first and also to the Greek. For in it the righteousness of God is revealed through faith for faith; as it is written, "The one who is righteous will live by faith."

Romans 1:16-17

Theological Thoughts

"Give us lips to sing Thy glory, Tongues Thy mercy to proclaim, Throats that shout the hope that fills us, Mouths to speak Thy holy name."[46]

ELW 511

Silence for Meditation

Psalm Fragment

Let the words of my mouth and the meditation of my heart be acceptable to you, O Lord, my rock and my redeemer.

Psalm 19:14

Questions to Ponder

· How do you feel when you receive Holy Communion?
· What does it look like to love one another as Jesus loves us?
· Does thinking of God's grace as our inheritance give you any new insights?

Prayer for Today

Jesus, thank you for entrusting us with this rich inheritance to share with others. Amen.

Day 39—Good Friday

> *But the righteousness that comes from faith says, "Do not say in your heart, 'Who will ascend into heaven?'" (that is, to bring Christ down) "or 'Who will descend into the abyss?'" (that is, to bring Christ up from the dead).*
> Romans 10:6-7

Do you remember the old children's song "We are climbing Jacob's ladder. . . . Ev'ry round goes higher, higher"? It's not really an accurate portrayal of the biblical story (Genesis 28:10-17). In Jacob's dream, the ladder between earth and heaven is not put there for Jacob to climb. It's the angels who are ascending and descending the ladder. And when the Lord speaks to Jacob in the dream, it's from right next to him. Yet for some reason, in our mental pictures of the story, we're the ones doing the climbing, up to heaven.

If we think of religion as *our* moving closer to God, we miss the central Christian witness: God in Christ comes down to us! In the incarnation, God in Christ meets humanity where we are. On the cross, God in Christ takes our place, offering his own life for our salvation. On the first Easter evening, the risen Christ comes through locked doors to comfort his frightened disciples. In the waters of baptism and in the bread and wine of Holy Communion, God in Christ comes to us to claim us, to cleanse us, and to nurture us for new life.

If we want to see God at work, the clearest place to look is on the cross of Good Friday. We refer to Jesus' suffering and death as "the passion," but it is hardly passive! Jesus actively chooses to take the cup offered to him in the garden of Gethsemane. Jesus actively chooses to carry the cross. Jesus actively chooses not to come down from the cross, although he is mocked for not doing so. Jesus actively chooses life—for us—at the cost of his own life. There's an old saying, "God's in his heaven and all's well with the world," but that's another version of the "up religion" that Luther called a theology of glory. The more faithful Christian confession is this: "God's down here with us, getting his hands dirty, getting his hands nailed to a cross, precisely because all's not well with the world."

But it will be. We call this Friday "good" because we trust the promise that God in Christ holds the whole world in his wounded hands.

Biblical Wisdom
For I am convinced that neither death, nor life, nor angels, nor rulers, nor things present, nor things to come, nor powers, nor height, nor depth, nor anything else in all creation, will be able to separate us from the love of God in Christ Jesus our Lord.
Romans 8:38-39

Theological Thoughts
"The only satisfying answer is the answer given to Job—the answer that is no answer but is the presence of an Answerer. It does not matter that the Answerer brings more questions than answers; for the answer is not the words as such but the living Word—the Presence itself."[47]
Douglas John Hall

Silence for Meditation

Psalm Fragment
My soul languishes for your salvation;
I hope in your word.
Psalm 119:81

Questions to Ponder
- Why did God become incarnate?
- Why did Jesus die?
- Why did Jesus descend into hell?

Prayer for Today
"On my heart imprint your image, blessed Jesus, king of grace. . . . Let the clear inscription be: Jesus, crucified for me, is my life, my hope's foundation, all my glory and salvation!"[48] Amen.
Thomas H. Kingo, ELW 811

Day 40—Holy Saturday

So faith comes from what is heard, and what is heard comes through the word of Christ.
     Romans 10:17

During the Easter season, when we hear the lessons in which Jesus appears to his disciples and sends them forth as witnesses of the resurrection, the meaning of Romans 10 seems obvious: we've heard the good news, and now we are sent out to share it with others.

But today is a day of silence, a day of waiting, a day of listening expectantly. Today, Holy Saturday, Jesus still lies buried in the tomb. As Christians, we have the advantage of knowing what we're waiting for—resurrection—but we still have to wait for it.

On the Sunday before Lent begins, some congregations observe the tradition of "burying the alleluia." That word of praise and rejoicing is set aside for the season of Lent and will not be said or sung in worship until Easter. Some congregations do not have flowers in the chancel during Lent. They may have green plants or nothing at all. Both traditions reinforce the sense that the Lenten season is a time of restraint. These traditions also help us learn to wait expectantly. We know that the flowers and alleluias will return. On Easter, the church will be filled with joyous sights and sounds. Because of our Lenten restraint, because we have been waiting so long, our Easter-lily, alleluia joy will be even greater.

Peter, James, and John spent Thursday night waiting in the garden of Gethsemane while Jesus prayed. Of course, they weren't very good at waiting. They kept falling asleep, and Jesus kept having to wake them. Today is our day of waiting. As Christians who live on this side of the resurrection, we know what we're waiting for. Our eyes and our ears are expectant, but we have to keep waiting. Sh. Be still, but don't fall asleep. Today is our day of waiting and listening, straining to hear the first sounds, the first words of Easter. Soon!

Biblical Wisdom
I am about to do a new thing; now it springs forth, do you not perceive it?
I will make a way in the wilderness and rivers in the desert.
> Isaiah 43:19

Theological Thoughts

"Resurrection, I tell them, comes on the third day, and it's something over which they have no control at all. . . . Their real job, therefore, in this second day of their lives is what the work of the second day always is: staying dead enough so resurrection can happen."[49]

Robert Farrar Capon

Silence for Meditation

Psalm Fragment
I wait for the LORD, my soul waits,
and in his word I hope.
> Psalm 130:5

Questions to Ponder

• How do you experience waiting? Does it make a difference when you know what you are waiting for?

• Does Lenten waiting for resurrection feel different from Advent waiting for Christmas?

More Questions to Ponder

As you reflect on your Lenten journey with the Word, when have you most clearly felt God's presence?

How will you continue journeying with the Word during the seven weeks of the Easter season?

Prayer for Today

Father, into your hands I commend my spirit. Amen.

Notes

1   *Luther's Works* [American edition], ed. Jaroslav Pelikan, Helmut T. Lehmann, and Hilton C. Oswald, 55 vols., (Philadelphia: Fortress Press; St. Louis: Concordia, 1955–1986), A Simple Way to Pray (1535), 43:198.

2   A Brief Instruction on What to Look for and Expect in the Gospels (1521), *LW* 31:121.

3   Paul Tillich, *Systematic Theology*, vol. 1 (Chicago: University of Chicago Press, 1951), 253.

4   Jaroslav Pelikan, *Jesus Through the Centuries* (New Haven and London: Yale University Press, 1985), 69.

5   Martin H. Franzmann, "Thy Strong Word," in *Evangelical Lutheran Worship* (Minneapolis: Augsburg Fortress, 2006), 511, stanza 6.

6   Lectures on Genesis: Chapters 1–5 (1535), *LW* 1:27.

7   Lectures on Genesis: Chapters 15–20 (1539), *LW* 3:274.

8   Dietrich Bonhoeffer, *Creation and Fall* (New York: Macmillan, 1959), 26.

9   H. Richard Niebuhr, *The Meaning of Revelation* (New York: Macmillan, 1962), 59.

10 St. John of the Cross, in *Breakfast with the Saints*, ed. LaVonne Neff (Ann Arbor: Servant Publications, 1996), 86.

11 Preface to the Large Catechism, in *The Book of Concord: The Confessions of the Evangelical Lutheran Church*, ed. Robert Kolb and Timothy J. Wengert (Minneapolis: Fortress Press, 2000), 380.

12 John Henry Newman, "Divine Calls," in *Callings*, ed. William C. Placher (Grand Rapids, Mich.: Eerdmans, 2005), 346.

13 Dietrich Bonhoeffer, *Cost of Discipleship* (New York: Macmillan, 1963), 87.

14 Bonhoeffer, *Cost of Discipleship*, 99.

15 Amy Plantinga Pauw, "Dying Well," in *Practicing Our Faith* (San Francisco: Jossey-Bass, 1997), 170.

16 Martin E. Marty, *Being Good and Doing Good* (Philadelphia: Fortress Press, 1984), 103.

17 The Freedom of a Christian (1520), *LW* 31:343.

18 The Large Catechism, *The Book of Concord*, 386.

19 Dorothy Bass, "Keeping Sabbath," in *Practicing Our Faith*, 78–79.

20 Saint Augustine, *Confessions*, trans. R.S. Pine Coffin (Harmondsworth, Middlesex, England: Penguin Books, 1961), 21.

21 Heidelberg Disputation (1518), *LW* 31:41.

22 Defense and Explanation of All the Articles (1521), *LW* 32:24.

23 Dietrich Bonhoeffer, *Life Together* (San Francisco: Harper & Row, 1954), 71.

24 St. Symeon the New Theologian, in *Breakfast with the Saints*, 134.

25 *ELW* 511, stanza 1.

26 Martin Franzmann, "O God, O Lord of Heaven and Earth," in *Lutheran Book of Worship* (Minneapolis: Augsburg Publishing House; Philadelphia: Board of Publication, Lutheran Church in America, 1978), 396, stanza 1.

27 Catherine of Siena, *A Life of Total Prayer: Selected Writings of Catherine of Siena* (Nashville: Upper Room Books, 2000), 49.

28 *ELW* 511, stanza 3.

29 St. Proclus, in *Breakfast with the Saints*, 127.

30   Harry Emerson Fosdick, "God of Grace and God of Glory," *ELW* 705, stanzas 1 and 4.

31   *Julian of Norwich: Showings*, trans. Edmund Colledge and James Walsh (New York: Paulist Press, 1978), 298.

32   The Lord's Prayer, The Second Petition, Small Catechism, in *The Book of Concord*, 356.

33   Krister Stendahl, *Meanings* (Philadelphia: Fortress Press, 1984), 234–235.

34   *ELW* 511, stanza 4.

35   St. Irenaeus of Lyons, in *Breakfast with the Saints*, 72.

36   Bonhoeffer, *Life Together*, 79.

37   Eight Sermons at Wittenberg (1522), *LW* 51:77.

38   A Brief Instruction on What to Look for and Expect in the Gospels (1521), *LW* 35:119.

39   Bonhoeffer, *Cost of Discipleship*, 155.

40   *ELW* 511, stanza 2.

41   Roberta C. Bondi, *A Place to Pray: Reflections on the Lord's Prayer* (Nashville: Abingdon, 1998), 116.

42   Kathryn A. Kleinhans, "Scriptural Authority," in *Talking Together as Christians about Homosexuality: A Guide for Congregations* (Chicago: Evangelical Lutheran Church in America Division for Church in Society, 1999), 47–48.

43   St. Nicodemos of the Holy Mountain, in *Breakfast with the Saints*, 114.

44   *The Desert Fathers: Sayings of the Early Christian Monks*, trans. Benedicta Ward (London: Penguin, 2003), 191.

45   Frances R. Havergal, "Lord, Speak to Us, That We May Speak," *ELW* 676, stanzas 1 and 2.

46   *ELW* 511, stanza 5.

47 Douglas John Hall, *God & Human Suffering* (Minneapolis: Augsburg, 1986), 118.

48 Thomas H. Kingo, "On My Heart Imprint Your Image," *ELW* 811.

49 Robert Farrar Capon, *Second Day* (New York: William Morrow, 1980), 143.